Series Editor Dale Gunthorp
Editor Susan Ward
Design Patrick Frean
Picture Research Maggie Colbeck
Production Philip Hughes
Consultants Marilyn Awoonor-Renner
　　　　　　　Raph Uwechue
Illustrations Ron Hayward Associates
　　　　　　　Dennis Mallet
　　　　　　　Marilyn Day
　　　　　　　Tony Payne
Maps Matthews and Taylor Associates

The **endpaper picture** shows a waterhole on the outskirts of Kano, norther Nigeria. It is a dry, dusty region, where water is scarce, and places such as this are natural gathering spots for washing, dipping, and just plain talking.

Page 6, Market day in Ibadan. "Market day" is rather a misleading term, since every day is market day in Nigeria. The "market mammies" of the south and their male Hausa compatriots in the north do a thriving business in everything from love potions to hot peppers, and even the "new Nigeria" in the background cannot displace the charm of the old.

Photographic sources Key to positions of illustrations: *(T)* top, *(C)* centre, *(B)* bottom, *(L)* left, *(R)* right. Associated Press: *47(CL)* British Museum: *41(TR)* Cash, J. Alan: *10(R)*, *13(TL)*, *23(BL) (BR)*, *27(BL)*, *28(BR)*, *29(BR)*, *35(TR) (BR)*, *38(TL)*, *41(TL)*, *51(BR)*, *53(TR) (BR)* Edwards, Mark: *20(TL)*, *28(BL)* FPG: *23(TL)* Forman, Werner: *40(BC)*, *40-41(BC)*, *44(BR)* Harding, Robert (Associates): *36-7(BC)* Hutchison, Alan: *8(TL)*, *10(B)*, *13(BR)*, *14(BC)*, *14-5(BC)*, *17(TC)*, *19(BC)*, *27(BR)*, *33(BR)*, *52(TC)* Keystone: *46(BR)* Mansell Collection: *42(BL) (BR)*, *45(CL) (TR)* Milsome, C: *13(C)* Moore, Dennis: *8(TL) (BL)*, *10(TL)*, *12-13(TC)*, *15(TR) (BR) (BL)*, *16(BR)*, *17(BC)*, *18(TL)*, *19(TR) (BR)*, *20-1(BC)*, *21(BR)*, *22(TC)*, *23(CR)*, *25(BL) (BR) (TR)*, *26-7(TC)*, *27(TC)*, *28(TL)*, *29(TL)*, *31(TL)*, *(TR) (BR) (CL)*, *33(BL) (TR)*, *34(TC)*, *35(BL)*, *36(BC)*, *37(TL) (BR)*, *38(BL) (CR)*, *39(TR) (BL) (BR)*, *45(BL) (BR)*, *51(BL)*, *52-3(BC)* Nigerian Embassy: *12(BR)*, *18(BL)*, *46(TC)*, *47(BR)*, *49(BL)*, *52(BC)* Pictor: *16(TC)*, *34(BC)* Radio Times (Hulton) Picture Library: *43(TR)* Royal Commonwealth Society: *43(BR)* SEF: *24(BL)*, *33(TL)* Sotheby's: *12(BC)* Synge, Richard: *25(TL)* Wilmer, Valerie: *32(BR)*, *49(TL) (BR)*.

First published 1975
Macdonald & Co (Publishers) Limited,
St Giles House, 49-50 Poland Street
London W1A 2LG
© Macdonald & Co (Publishers)
Limited 1975
ISBN 0 356 05101 3

Made and printed by
Morrison & Gibb Limited
Edinburgh, Scotland

Colour reproduction by
Fotomecanica Iberia, Madrid

Nigeria

the land and its people

Richard Synge

Macdonald Educational

Contents

8 Many peoples, one nation

10 Forests, rivers and savannahs

12 The Nigerian influence

14 Family life

16 Fashion, Nigerian style

18 Sports and pastimes

20 Language and communication

22 Education

24 A religious society

26 Customs and superstitions

28 The market

30 Eating the Nigerian way

32 Life set to music

34 Arts and crafts

36 Getting around in Nigeria

38 City life—Lagos and Kano

40 A proud past

42 God, glory—and slaves

44 The march of colonialism

46 Independence and civil war

48 Heroes in fact and fiction

50 The Nigerian character

52 A nation on the move

54 Reference: Geography and Government

56 Reference: History and the Arts

58 Reference: the Economy

60 Gazetteer

61 Index

62 Political map of Nigeria

63 Physical map of Nigeria

Many peoples, one nation

▲ Carved ivory leopard from the royal palace in Benin. The first Europeans to see Benin, in 1472, were impressed by its organization and power.

New and old

Nigeria is a young country. Its boundaries were drawn by Britain in 1900 and it has been independent only since 1960. But each of its many different ethnic groups (or 'tribes') has its own long history and a rich and exciting culture.

The earliest inhabitants of the area now known as Nigeria probably arrived before 3000 BC. These people left neolithic axes and mysterious rock paintings which are still discovered all over the country. The first Nigerian civilisation we know about is called the 'Nok culture'. It flourished in the plateau region north of the river Benue before the time of Christ: its people have left behind fine clay sculptures and evidence that they developed iron-working techniques.

In the centuries before 1000 AD, the area of modern Nigeria was the focal point of many important population movements in Africa. Migrations from the Sahara (which was once green) and the Red Sea pushed from the north and east introducing Arabic or Hamitic racial types, while people of pure Negro stock are thought to have spread into Central Africa from southern Nigeria. Powerful empires had been established by the time these migrations stopped.

Land of many kingdoms

A static population brought greater stability. Even today rulers of these old kingdoms still have ceremonial authority.

The longest surviving empire was Kanem-Borno, which dominated the Lake Chad area for a thousand years. The northern city states of the Hausa people have also had great trading influence for centuries.

In the southwest the Yoruba people developed from the sophisticated 12th century culture of Ife which, like the kingdom of Benin, produced some of the most creative and vivid art in all Africa. The Ibos of the southeast had a different system, living in democratically-ruled village communities, farming and trading peaceably.

Altogether Nigeria boasts about 250 different ethnic groups, with different languages, cultures and life-styles. Only in this century have they been forced to live together under one political system and, understandably, there have been many problems. The most populous groups have feared each other, while the small groups have felt dominated by the large ones. These tensions led to a terrible civil war, but nowadays there is a real feeling of peace and progress as the people learn to think of themselves as united Nigerians.

Ethnic groups
Who, where and how many?

Nigeria's largest ethnic groups are the Hausa in the north, the Yoruba in the southwest and the Ibo in the southeast. All of these areas include smaller tribes. The northern Fulani are nomadic cattlemen, well versed in Islam.

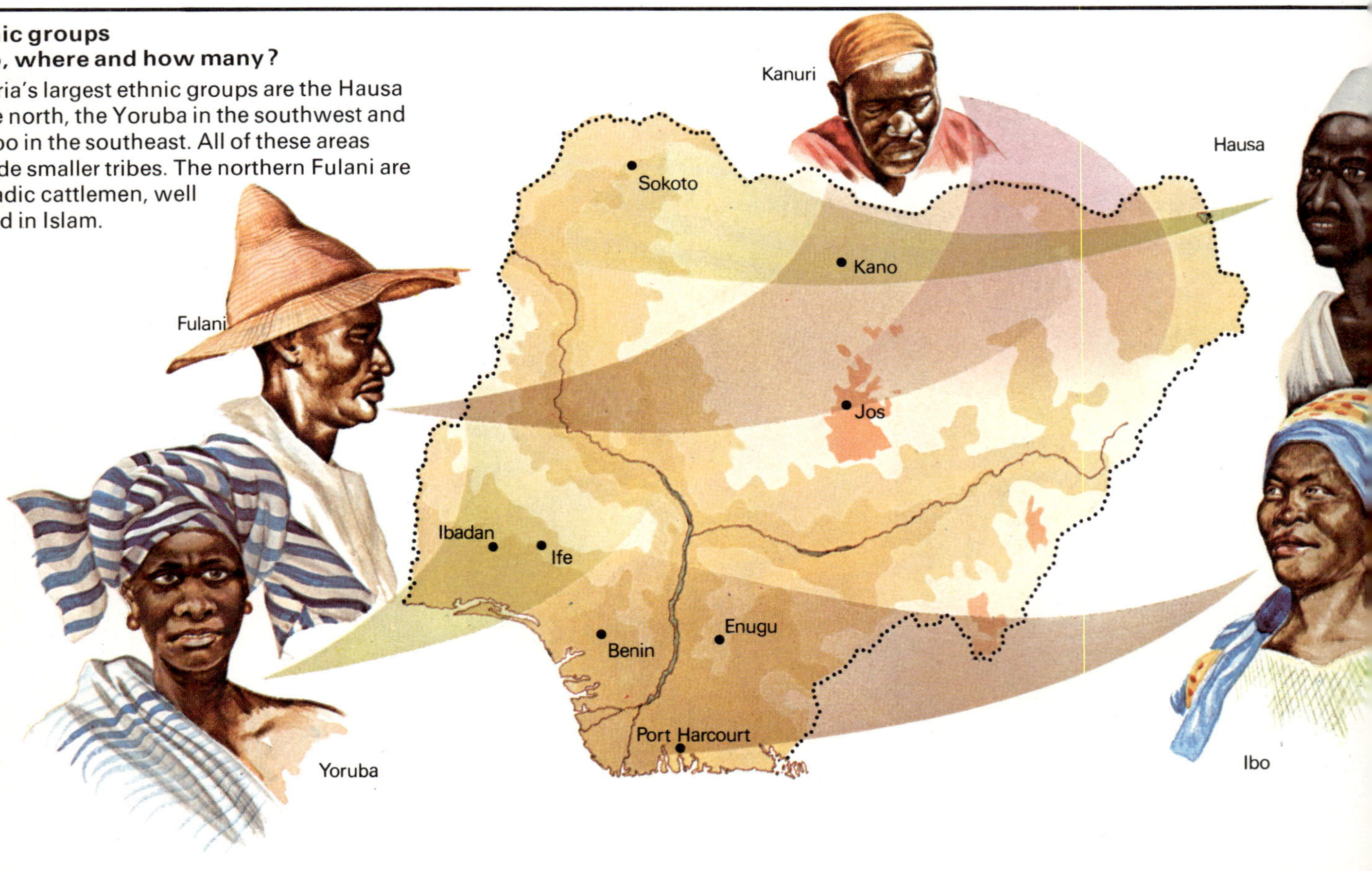

Kanuri

Hausa

Sokoto

Kano

Fulani

Jos

Ibadan

Ife

Benin

Enugu

Port Harcourt

Yoruba

Ibo

▲ The face of Nigeria—a detail of a crowd in Lagos. Like any large city, Lagos has acted as a lodestone, attracting people from all over the country.

▼ Nigerians love to dress colourfully, wearing both traditional and modern styles. Golfing umbrellas keep out the rain, ward off the sun and, most important, attract attention. This man is also wearing a typical Yoruba-style cap.

▼ Modern architecture in Ibadan, Western State. Nigeria is a rapidly developing country with facilities for modern administration and communication.

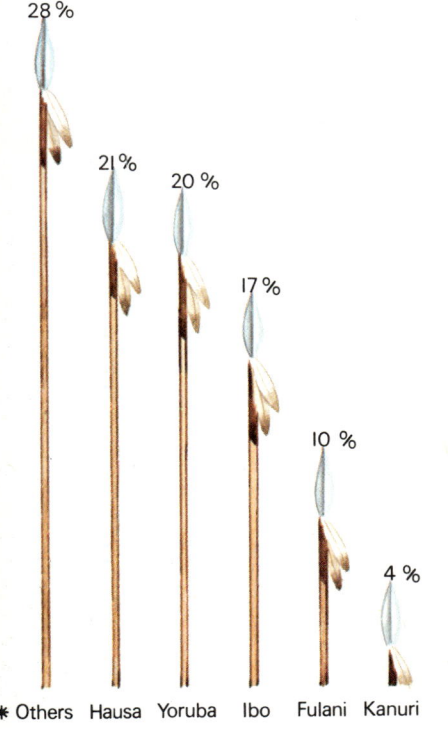

28 %

21 %

20 %

17 %

10 %

4 %

✳ Others Hausa Yoruba Ibo Fulani Kanuri

✳ 'Others' includes members of all smaller tribes, i.e. Ibibio, Nupe, Tiv, Edo, etc.

Based on 1973 census estimates.

9

Forests, rivers and savannahs

Great variety

Nigeria has as much variety of terrain and climate as it does of people. It lies in the tropics covering an area of 356,669 sq. miles. Different geographical belts traverse the country laterally.

The low-lying coastal area is a hot and humid zone of mangrove swamps broken up by a network of lagoons, creeks and rivers. The coast itself has endless white beaches.

The biggest feature of the southern belt is the huge sprawling delta of the Niger River, the main lifeline of West Africa. Rising in Guinea, the Niger flows through semi-desert and enters Nigeria in the northwest.

Thick tropical rain forest extends inland for up to 100 miles. It once extended even further inland, but much has been cleared to make way for farming land. Grassy savannah, alternating with tree-covered parkland, is the main feature of the 'middle belt'.

Highlands and plains

Everywhere in Nigeria the land rolls gently. It rises sharply only at the Jos Plateau and along the border with Cameroon. These highland areas have a pleasantly dry and cool climate. They provide a popular holiday retreat, away from the intense heat of the rest of the country.

The very north of Nigeria reaches into the semi-desert zone known as the Sahel, where the terrible drought of 1972 and 1973 caused people to think the Sahara desert was advancing into Nigeria.

All over Nigeria the main activity of the people is farming. Each area has crops suited to the climate—cattle thrive only on higher ground, away from tsetse fly.

▲ Fulani cattlemen travel far and wide through Nigeria and the whole of West Africa to find good pasture for their animals. The open plains of the north are perfect for this style of life, to which the Fulani adhere proudly.

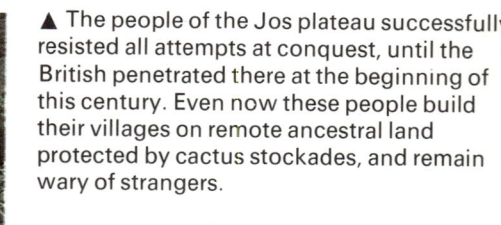

▲ The people of the Jos plateau successfully resisted all attempts at conquest, until the British penetrated there at the beginning of this century. Even now these people build their villages on remote ancestral land protected by cactus stockades, and remain wary of strangers.

◀ A village on the river Niger. The delta area has a hostile climate and dense vegetation. Europeans were trading for ivory and slaves in these parts for centuries before they realized that the complex of lagoons, creeks and swamps was in fact the mouth of the vast Niger, Africa's third longest river. The first Europeans to discover the river's course were the Lander brothers, in the year 1830.

A land of contrasts

The varying types of terrain and climate have led Nigerians to adopt the most suitable and convenient materials and designs for their houses. History has also played its part. Zaria, for example, has long been an important commercial centre with fine houses and streets, while Lagos—with its good harbour and centuries of contact with Europe—is the natural capital of modern Nigeria.

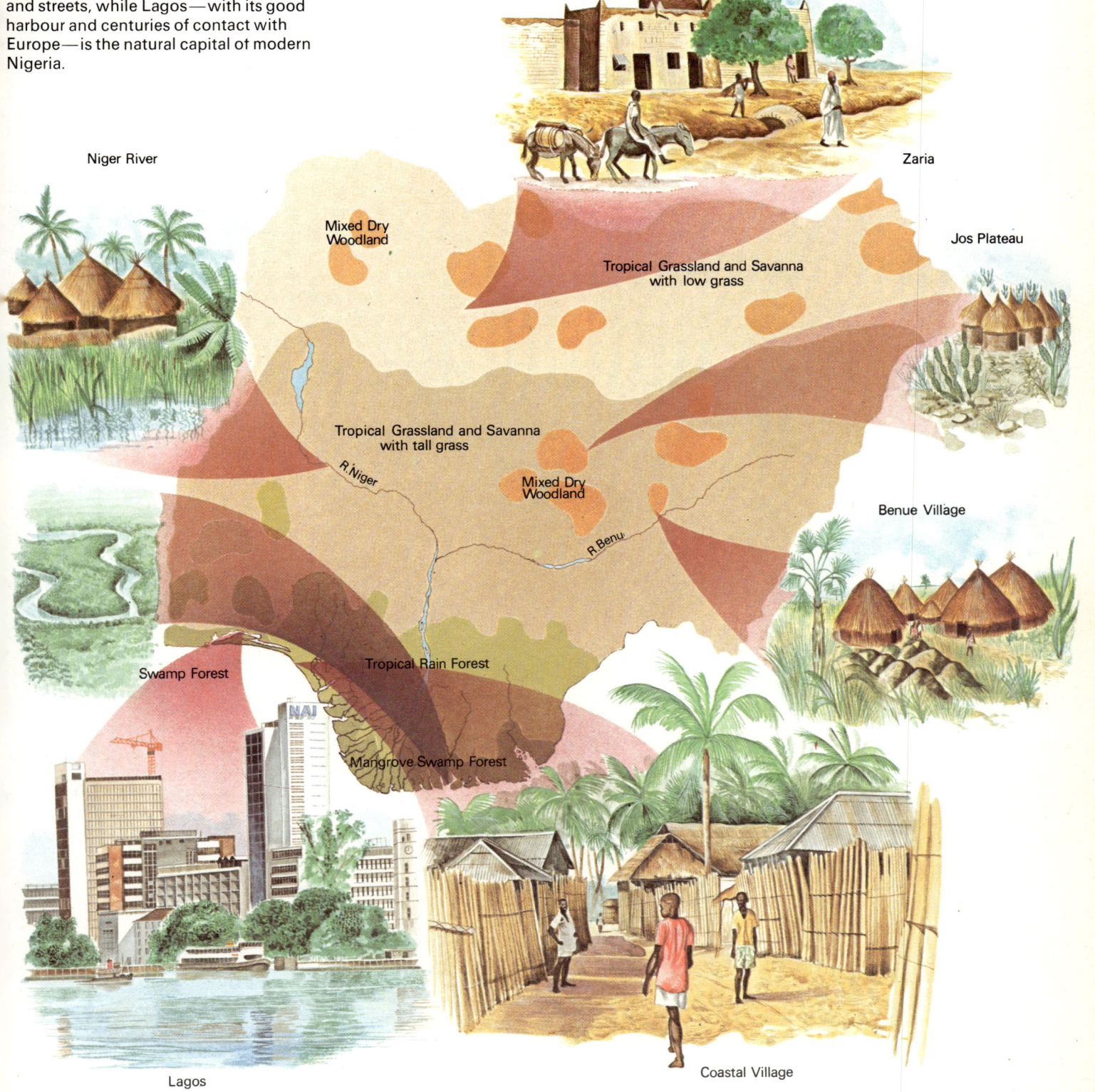

Niger River

Zaria

Mixed Dry Woodland

Jos Plateau

Tropical Grassland and Savanna with low grass

Tropical Grassland and Savanna with tall grass

R. Niger

Mixed Dry Woodland

R. Benu

Benue Village

Swamp Forest

Tropical Rain Forest

Mangrove Swamp Forest

Lagos

Coastal Village

11

The Nigerian influence

A nation of traders

Now, as in the past, the influence of Nigeria is primarily commercial. Even before the Europeans arrived, Kano and the Hausa city-states acted as a bridge between North Africa and the forest peoples of the south, while the Kanem-Borno empire controlled slave trading across the eastern Sahara.

When European traders arrived on the coast after the fifteenth century, some states grew rich and powerful through providing for the foreigners' needs—whether ivory or slaves. The slave-ship captains thought they were taking nothing more than cheap labour over the Atlantic; they did not realise they were taking people with a rich culture. Although this culture was nearly destroyed in the misery of the plantations, West African music survived as the basis of rock-and-roll, jazz, soul and other American music.

Nigeria now has many successful traders, not just in its own markets, but all over West and Central Africa. Nigerians are also doing business in Europe and the Americas.

A huge population

Nigeria has the largest population of any country in Africa, approaching 80 million. Thus it provides an important market for foreign goods. The old towns and cities are growing rapidly with the expansion of industry and transport.

Because of its new-found wealth from oil Nigeria has great influence in Africa and the world, and often acts as a spokesman on African affairs. It also has great military strength, although there is no intention of using this against outsiders.

New roads are being built across Africa, from north to south and from east to west. Nigeria is at the hub of all these routes and will soon be in a position to dominate much of the continent economically, educationally and culturally. The money from oil is being put to good use in building new industries and an excellent educational system. It also enables Nigeria to stage lavish sports and cultural events. When more hotels are built it could become a popular tourist centre too.

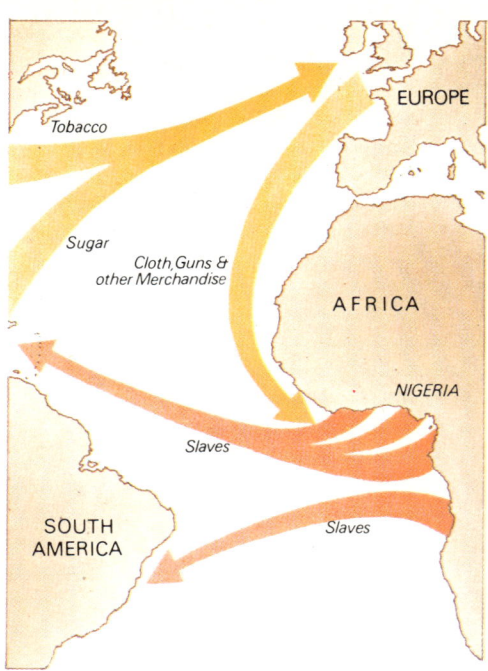

▲ The 'triangular trade' that made slavery so profitable for English merchants and put Nigeria on the Europeans' maps for the first time—under the generalised name 'Benin'.

▲ Art dealers all over the world crave genuine Benin bronzes like this one, sold at Sotheby's, London for £85,000 in 1974. Most of the treasures from Benin's royal palace are now in the British Museum.

▲ When groundnuts (or peanuts) are gathered and bagged ready for export, they are stacked in pyramids like this.

▼ General Gowon (right), Nigeria's Head of State, welcoming the President of Sierra Leone at a conference of the Organisation of African Unity.

► Where Nigerians travel and what they do. There are Nigerian trading communities in many parts of Africa, and increasing numbers of Nigerians travel overseas to study.

▼ Nigeria is now brought closer to the outside world by air transport, as this sign at Kano airport shows. Many international flights stop here, thus continuing Kano's place in world commerce. As many as 50,000 Nigerian Muslims fly to Mecca from Kano every year for the annual pilgrimage, known as the *Hajj*.

Where they go

Africa: traders, businessmen, diplomats, teachers, doctors and lawyers.

Britain: students, nurses, doctors, lawyers, clerical workers and businessmen.

U.S.A.: students, academics, writers and businessmen.

Western Europe: diplomats, students, businessmen and engineers.

U.S.S.R.: students of engineering, medicine, and practical sciences.

A supplier for modern demands

Where most of Nigeria's exports go (according to 1972 statistics).

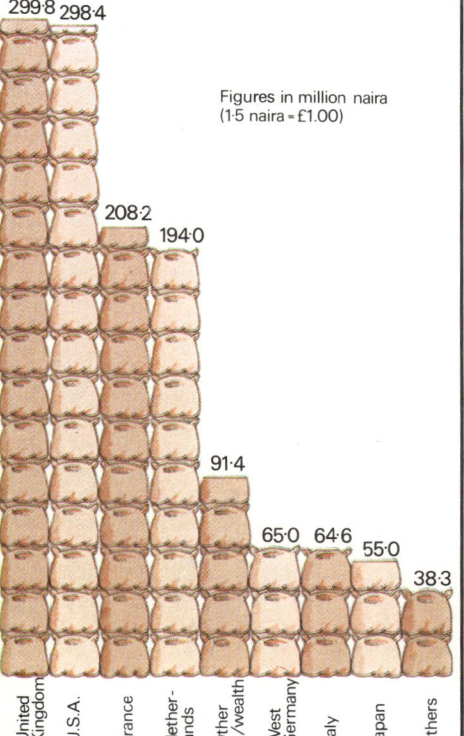

Figures in million naira (1·5 naira = £1.00)

299·8 298·4 — United Kingdom, U.S.A.
208·2 — France
194·0 — Netherlands
91·4 — Other C/wealth
65·0 — West Germany
64·6 — Italy
55·0 — Japan
38·3 — Others

► Oil was discovered off Nigeria's shore in the late 1950s. It has now been developed to such an extent that Nigeria is Africa's biggest producer. Output is expected to reach three million barrels a day by 1980, but after that it may begin to decline.

Family life

The extended family

As in all of black Africa, Nigerian families extend beyond the immediate next of kin to include the most distant relatives as 'brothers and sisters'. In village life there is a harmonious communal existence, but in towns too the households are often large.

Old people are looked after without question and indeed are respected above all other members of the family for their wisdom and experience. The elders of a village decide all matters of importance. Things that are by rights the property of a whole village are shared out from the eldest downwards.

Children are brought up by a whole 'extended family' and not just by their parents. They thus become familiar with the traditions and rules from a very early age.

In village life there is communal ownership of land and this gives every member of a village great security. Unfortunately all the traditional ways of organizing society are giving way to Western influence. Families are beginning to 'shrink'.

Marriage

Traditionally a man could marry as many women as he could afford, but this practice is beginning to die out. A man would pay a bride-price for each wife; this usually kept the number of wives to a manageable level. If a new wife was unhappy with her husband she was free to leave him but would have to return the bride-price in full before she could remarry.

There are now four types of marriage in Nigeria: 1. Registry Office 2. Christian 3. Muslim 4. Native Law and Custom. The first three are the same as practised elsewhere in the world, while the fourth is decided by the traditional elders and authorities in each locality. The traditional way might seem to degrade women, but in fact it gives them more rights and independence than does the Muslim or the Christian way. African women, however, do an enormous amount of physical labour in the home, in the fields and in the market, while their husbands try to find paid labour in the towns.

A day in the life of a farming family. The day begins as the sun rises. Mother prepares a breakfast of corn or porridge. She then takes her baby to the fields, planting while father tends the animals and the children leave for school. In the mid-afternoon mother returns home, collecting firewood and water for the evening meal. Father discusses village affairs with the other men. After washing up, everyone goes to bed.

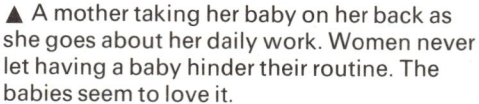

▲ A mother taking her baby on her back as she goes about her daily work. Women never let having a baby hinder their routine. The babies seem to love it.

▲ Fulani villagers preparing food in their family compound, northern Nigeria. The men of the village are out tending their herds of cattle.

▼ These women in the Mid-West State go to the village well not only to wash clothes and draw water, but to trade local gossip. Even in the main towns only a minority of homes have their own running water.

▲ Like any Western family scene, these urban Nigerians are looking at family snapshots in their comfortable bungalow in Lagos.

◄ Poorer town families live in communal housing compounds like this one in Benin. Each family group has different quarters.

▼ A typical suburban home for a middle-class family. The husband has a white-collar job, and finds a car is essential for his way of life.

Fashion Nigerian style

▲ Yoruba man and woman in colourful traditional clothing for special occasions.

◄ An Ibo man in traditional costume. The light cotton fabric is a modern print.

▲ Yoruba drummer wearing printed cotton tunic and trousers.

▲ A Kanuri girl wearing one of the many hairstyles found in north eastern Nigeria. On her head is a calabash. Her beads are of glass, made by local craftsmen.

► A weaver from Ilorin displaying his intricately worked cloth.

▲ Hausa retainers to a northern Emir (nobleman) wearing ceremonial costume.

Changing styles

Before Europeans arrived every ethnic group had its own distinctive costume. Recently there have been many adaptations and changes, but on the whole Nigerians are fiercely proud of their traditional clothing. Although work in modern offices and industries demands something more streamlined than a flowing gown, many Nigerians change into national costume for relaxation after a day in suit and tie. Outside the towns traditional garb is normal.

A love of colour

The Yoruba wear colourful gowns (*agbada*) and caps. Indigo cloth is a traditional material but now modern dyes and prints abound. The Hausa also wear gowns and caps, but in dazzling white unless they are people of influence. These wear gowns of a single colour with embroidered patterns. Hausa festive dress presents a dazzling array of colours.

All over Nigeria women wear brightly printed fabrics, arranged in a variety of styles, but always without using pins, zips or buttons. Their headress is usually of matching material and arranged in equally complicated folds.

Tailoring is an important industry both for traditional and modern clothing.

▲ A Hausa in an expensive tribal robe which, despite its plain colour, is finely stitched and embroidered in symbolic patterns.

▲ Brightly coloured horsemen in the Hausa city of Katsina celebrate the Muslim Sallah festival.

▼ Benin women at a Western-style wedding show how cleverly old styles adapt to the whims of fashion.

Fashion that goes to the head

A popular hairstyle among Nigerian girls sometimes known as the "medusa".

A traditional intricate hairstyle worn by village women in the northeast.

A Yoruba girl in a turban known as *asoi-oke*, held in place without any pins.

A Fulani woman in a simply combed and parted hairstyle, common all over the country.

17

Sports and pastimes

▼ These men are playing *Ayo*, a version of a game popular all over Africa. It consists of moving seeds around the board in a predetermined fashion, rather like backgammon. It can also be played on the ground with holes scooped out of the earth.

Sport and drama

In past times Nigerians used to have their own 'sporting seasons' after harvesting their crops. Sports included wrestling, archery, hunting, racing, swimming, fishing competitions, canoe racing, horse racing and acrobatics.

Music and drama were also important leisure activities at any time of the year. Africans' love of drumming, singing and dancing is well known, but they have an equal enthusiasm for story-telling and acting, which is always done with complete audience participation. Even when they watch modern films, especially Westerns, Nigerian audiences take sides with the characters and applaud their every move.

Love of football

Since the Europeans arrived a whole new range of sports have been enthusiastically adopted by Nigerians. Football is a particular favourite since it is played by school-

▲ Drummers at a rehearsal for the Festival of Black and African Arts Culture held in 1975. Over 90 countries from five continents participate.

▶ Some of the modern sports now popular in Nigeria. There are more and more excellent athletes and facilities to accommodate them.

children from an early age. Officially there is no professional football, but a number of companies employ sportsmen and give them training facilities so as to boost the sport (and give the company a good name).

Other European sports with a keen following in Nigeria are: cricket, athletics, table tennis, lawn tennis, boxing, hockey, basketball and polo. At one time only the British colonial officers were interested in polo, or could afford to play, but it has caught on with the ruling elite.

Local festivals take place in Nigeria throughout the year, according to custom. Behind their serious religious significance is a very basic desire for a good time every now and then. A festival has many component parts but it is always held together by music and dancing. In Lagos a fairly common sight is the Eyo Festival, a traditional street play staged in memory of prominent citizens or to celebrate some important event.

▲ Men and women dance in their separate groups at local festivals. A ceremony in Lagos is an occasion—and an excuse—for merry-making.

▼ The dream of almost all schoolboys is to play on the national team of Nigeria. They seize every opportunity to kick a ball around on a piece of waste ground.

▲ The opening ceremony of the All-Africa Games held in Lagos in 1973. Nigerian athletes came second in the Games, after the Egyptians. The huge stadium was built especially for the event and Nigeria hopes that one day it will be considered as a venue for the Olympic Games. There are already many Nigerian athletes competing and winning medals in international events around the world.

Language and communication

▼ There are many lively daily newspapers, mainly in English, and plenty of weeklies and monthlies, varying from popular feature and sports subjects to hard news.

The importance of English

The multitude of Nigeria's original languages has made it difficult for its leaders to decide on one acceptable national language. There are four basic groups of language (Kanuri, Hausa, Bantu and Yoruba/Ido Ibo) but at present the most widely known language for the whole nation is English—in official and pidgin form. Pidgin English originated as a trading language in Calaba in the sixteenth century.

English is the language of Government education and the newspapers. Despite it connection with colonialism, English now a force for unity among Nigeria' diverse peoples and it also opens Nigeria' doors to the world.

Although there is a military Government the newspapers have more freedom to criticise than in almost any other African country.

Literature

Original Nigerian literature was spoke and not written. It consisted of fable legends, history, poetry and imaginative story-telling. Singing played an important part in literary 'performances', which fortunately still thrive in villages and towns.

In the last twenty-five years man Nigerians have turned their hand to writing, both to preserve the old stories and to record the cultural conflicts of colonialism and independence. Some writers, like Wole Soyinka and Chinua Achebe, are famous abroad.

▼ The old means of communication in 'the bush' was by beating a hollowed tree trunk. The rhythm produced by this Tiv elder can be heard 20 miles away.

Typical radio programmes in a Nigerian day (examples from National Station)	
5:30a.m.	Drum signal
5:34	National anthem
5:40	Family prayers
5:50	Reading from the Holy Koran
6:03	From the Nigerian Editorials
8:03	News summaries in Edo, Efik, Fulfulde & Hausa
8:15	Mixed grill
8:30	Kiddies playtime
8:45	Light music from the Netherlands
9:00	News summaries in Ibo, Ijaw, Kanuri, Tiv and Yoruba.
9:15	Soul lift
10:30	Jingle hour
11:33	Hausa magazine
12:03p.m.	Music for dancing
2:03	Cultural echoes
4:15	For children
4:30	Negro College Choir
8:03	Lagos State news (English and Yoruba)
9:10	Muslim sermon

► Television has already reached most states in Nigeria. Only the rich can afford their own sets and so restaurants and bars often have sets for the benefit of their customers. Many of the programmes are imported, but local shows are improving.

a man of the people
by chinua achebe

◄ Greetings in Ibo, Yoruba, Hausa and Arabic (which is used by northerners, especially in their dealings with people from the Sahara and North Africa). The visitor may be confused by the vast number of different local greetings used by Nigerians among themselves. In some tribes each family has a completely different way of saying 'good morning'. Luckily nearly everyone understands plain 'Hello!' too.

▲ Part of a serialised novel by the famous Nigerian writer, Chinua Achebe. This passage is in pidgin—a fascinating language in its own right.

▼ Huge advertising hoardings dominate the roads in the main towns. The slogans are often in English, pidgin and local languages, which vary from region to region.

Education

Traditional teaching

When the European missionaries arrived in Nigeria they thought they were introducing education for the first time but they were wrong. Traditional education was a complex process that involved the teaching of history passed down by word of mouth. Legends, stories of heroism and parables all had to be memorized by heart, since writing was unknown. At the same time all children were taught agricultural skills, herding, hunting and handicrafts, and were taken to the fields or the forest with their family at an early age.

This perfectly natural form of education was designed to pass on values which were essential to community survival in the conditions that then existed. The highest values were hospitality, bravery, the dignity of labour and respect for the elders of the community.

In the Islamic north of Nigeria, education was more formal, with the use of the Arabic script and an emphasis on religion.

Education for all

British-style education was first started in the south and there are still more schools there than in the north. But the Government is determined to overcome the imbalance and to introduce free primary education for all children within a very short time.

Since independence, new Universities have been opening every few years to cope with the growing numbers of successful secondary school pupils who are determined to extend their education as far as they can. University campuses are now open at Lagos, Ibadan, Ile-Ife, Nsukka, Benin, Calabar, Zaria, Jos and Kano.

The Government is trying to involve young people in the development of the whole country and has launched a National Youth Service Corps which qualified students must join. They are sent to all parts of the country to teach, do medical work or organize voluntary labour. The young people who have worked for the Youth Service find that it has taught them much about their own country that they never knew before, and has helped them to overcome distrust of other tribes.

▲ Girls in a Government primary school. There is a problem of overcrowding in many schools but the Government is building many new classrooms and recruiting new teachers to cope with the situation.

The educational system

Koran schools   State schools   Private schools   Mission schools

15,000 Primary schools .... 4,000,000 pupils

State schools   Mission schools   Private schools

1,500 Secondary schools .... 400,000 pupils

Vocational, commercial & technical training 17,000 students (state & private)

6 State Universities 15,000 students

200 Teachers training colle 40,000 students

▲ The educational system in 1972, with government, private and mission schools working side by side. In a short time the vast majority of schools will be run by the government and the number of primary schools will have doubled, to cater for more than 10 million primary school pupils. Most of the new schools will be built in the North.

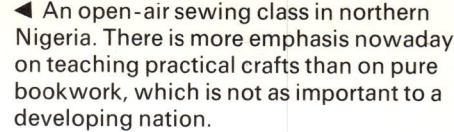
◀ An open-air sewing class in northern Nigeria. There is more emphasis nowadays on teaching practical crafts than on pure bookwork, which is not as important to a developing nation.

▼ This school meal is not as unappetising as it looks. African cooking—like that everywhere—suffers when it is prepared for large numbers of children.

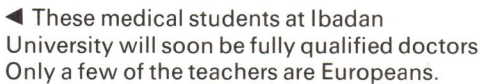
◀ These medical students at Ibadan University will soon be fully qualified doctors. Only a few of the teachers are Europeans.

▼ A scene at Ibadan University, which was founded after World War II and was the first full university in Nigeria.

A religious society

Spirit worship

In their traditional system Africans worshipped spirits who could protect them from the forces of chaos and destruction. Every tribe gave particular honour to its own ancestors, whose presence in the community was deeply felt. Many tribes had special gods who represented natural elements such as rain and thunder. These would have to be appeased at certain times so that they could help with the growing and harvesting of crops.

Above all the gods and spirits was the supreme creator who passed the life force through different channels, varying from tribe to tribe. Worship maintained a universal balance between man and nature and ensured the continued survival of the tribe. An important aspect was artistic expression through music, dancing and sculpture.

Christianity and Islam

European missionaries were determined to destroy the traditional beliefs which they saw as evil and primitive. They did not succeed completely although there are now many Christian sects in Nigeria. Some of these sects are a combination of Christianity and traditional beliefs.

Islam arrived in northern Nigeria around 1000 AD and has influenced every aspect of life there. In the nineteenth century the Fulani spread its hold even further.

▼ A blue-painted jester performs for the Emir—the traditional ruler of Kano—at a festival celebrating the end of Ramadan. On occasions such as this, the influence of ancient African beliefs on Islamic practice becomes particularly apparent.

Animist and spirit religions

Religion was the inspiration for all traditional art in Nigeria, especially in the making of masks. They had the power to take over the spirit of the wearer.

A *gelede* mask worn in an annual festival. It wards off evil spirits by making them laugh.

A royal Benin mask made of ivory. Designed to be suspended from the King's neck, it symbolizes his religious authority.

A stone figure carved to commemorate the head of a village of the Ekoi people, South-Eastern State.

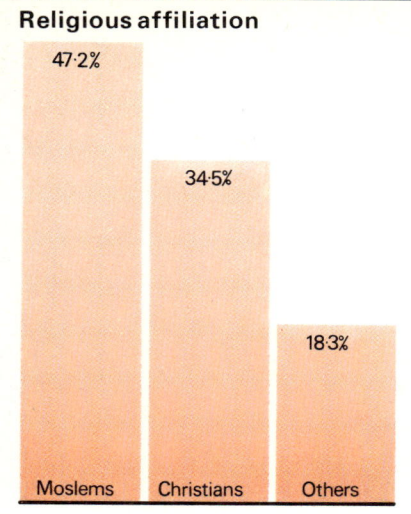

Religious affiliation

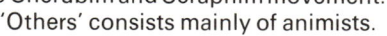

Islam is experiencing a more rapid growth in Africa than Christianity, though like Christianity it is divided into different sects. The centre of Islam in Nigeria is the city of Sokoto.

Nigerian Christians are divided into Catholics, Protestants and new breakaway groups. The latter are at present more successful at making converts. The fastest growing sect is the Cherubim and Seraphim movement. 'Others' consists mainly of animists.

▲ The large city mosque in Kano, built quite recently to cope with the increasing number of Muslims. On a Friday some 50,000 people crowd into and around the mosque.

▲ An Anglican church service identical to one in England. Some of the congregation are wearing Western clothes, and others, traditional costume.

▲ A preacher from a small Christian sect trying to find potential converts in the market place.

► A shrine in Benin in honour of different family and tribal gods. Animals are sometimes sacrificed here.

Customs and superstitions

Changing traditions

Nigerians have maintained many customs from the old day, but the emphasis on Western-style education and exposure to Christianity has caused the young to question many of their tribal beliefs. Despite this, some traditions survive longer than others. Hospitality is one of them and duty to the family is another, although it imposes heavy pressures on successful people. A rich man often finds himself responsible for the education and maintenance of a host of distant relatives whom he hardly knows. Nigerians who have been to Europe or the USA are also expected to come back with fast cars and pots of money. For this reason many Nigerians put off going home for as long as they can.

The most positive side of traditional custom has been retained in the form of festivals and dancing. There are also some ceremonies in the remote parts of the country which incorporate quite cruel customs. Tests of manhood among the Fulani involve the merciless beating of each young man of marrying age. If he shows no pain from the lashes of the birch he can marry the girl of his choice; he who fails can never marry.

Ghosts and demons

For people who lived in the forest, their family and their village was a secure world while everything outside in the dark forest was frightening and full of evil spirits. Spine-chilling stories would be told of ghosts and demons who lurked in the trees. A Yoruba writer, Amos Tutuola, has collected many of these tales into his books the best of which is *The Palm Wine Drinkard* (sic).

There were many degrees of misfortune that could befall people in the old days but none was as bad for the Yoruba as the death of twin children. If it ever happened there was an elaborate procedure to ensure that such bad luck never occurred again. Stylized wooden carvings were made by a master craftsman to represent the spirit of the twins. These were then worshipped and treated just like the real twins: washed, clothed and offered food each day.

▶ Hordes of men climb down the banks of one of the main tributaries of the Niger, at Argungu. This stretch of the river is only fished once a year when, in keeping with the custom of centuries, the Sultan of Sokoto presides over a great fishing competition.

▲ The custom of paying an agreed sum of money for a wife to her parents still persists, although nowadays the sum is usually a mere token to please the family ancestors.

▲ A Hausa doctor writes holy words from the Koran on a slate. They are then washed into a cup and drunk!

▼ A version of the West African handshake, used by young Nigerians to demonstrate friendship and brotherhood. Also used by black Americans.

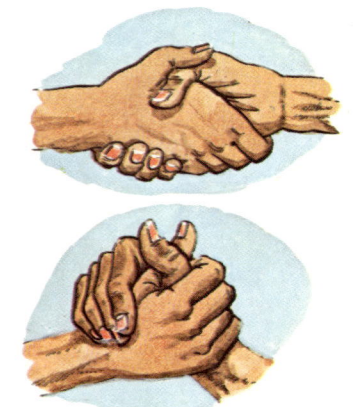

1

2

▲ Touching food with the left hand is considered the height of bad manners. The same applies to pointing.

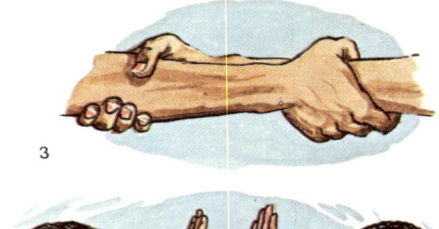

3

4

▲ Kola nuts. One is always offered to a guest as a sign of welcome. They are chewed slowly. The juice is very bitter in taste but the effect is stimulating.

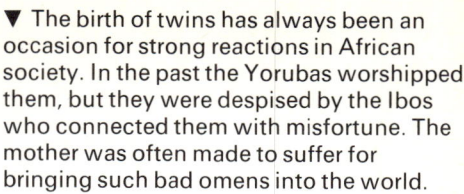

▼ The birth of twins has always been an occasion for strong reactions in African society. In the past the Yorubas worshipped them, but they were despised by the Ibos who connected them with misfortune. The mother was often made to suffer for bringing such bad omens into the world.

▼ In the past most Nigerian tribes had distinctive face markings, so that a stranger could immediately identify a man's clan and family. The incisions were made at birth.

▲ A witchcraft stall in Kano market. Nigerians still have great faith in their traditional doctors, who use all sorts of gimmicks to prove their prowess.

The market

▼ The food market in Ibadan, one of the biggest markets in West Africa. Ibadan is an important city because of the dominance of its traders in Yorubaland and neighbouring areas. The 'market mammies' rarely use standard weights and measures in their transactions but divide their goods into little piles.

Focus of Nigerian life

Nigeria's lifeblood has always been trade, and every other activity is subordinate to it. The big cities all grew around a central market. Today this draws from and serves the smaller village markets but also has contacts with nations abroad.

Some markets specialize in cloth, others in baskets, some in cattle, others in camels, but everywhere there is a centre for basic provisions: meat, fish, vegetables, fruit, spices, cooking oil etc. The large markets are open every day while the smaller ones open once a week, or every third or fifth day according to tradition.

Hives of activity

Whether in town or village the market provides a fascinating display of the requirements and amusements of the local inhabitants. Drummers, singers, pipe players and jugglers weave their way through the crowds, while old men hold earnest discussions on local politics and young men chat up the girls.

In the north the markets are run by men, but in the south it is the women who rule with an iron hand. The prosperity of these ladies gives them considerable social and political influence which they use with expert skill.

▼ The principal unit of Nigerian currency is the naira, which is divided into 100 Kobo. Until 1973 Nigeria used the old British currency of pounds, shillings and pence. One naira equals ten old shillings.

▲ Textiles are one of the biggest-selling items in Nigeria; lengths of cloth are the basic items of clothing in a hot climate.

▲ Although traditional soap is very effective, most housewives now use modern detergents for their laundry.

◄ Enamel pots and pans from Eastern Europe are very popular in the home because they are cheap, colourful and durable.

▲ Hot peppers on sale in Lagos. Although Lagos has many supermarkets and department stores, all fresh food is still sold in the old-fashioned markets from stalls. There are no greengrocers' or butchers' shops. You can buy bread in a bakery, but it is also sold by boys with trays on their heads.

► The camel market in Kano, where you would start or finish your journey if you planned to cross the Sahara the traditional way. If the Sahara is a sea of sand, then Kano is the great port of the desert and the camels are its ships. Sadly the great camel caravans are now giving way to lorries.

◄ Musicians always gather in the market place because they are sure of an audience. This is how apprentice musicians gain most of their experience, because they can gauge how well they are playing by the response from the crowd. The greatest praise is when traders stop their work to listen.

Eating the Nigerian way

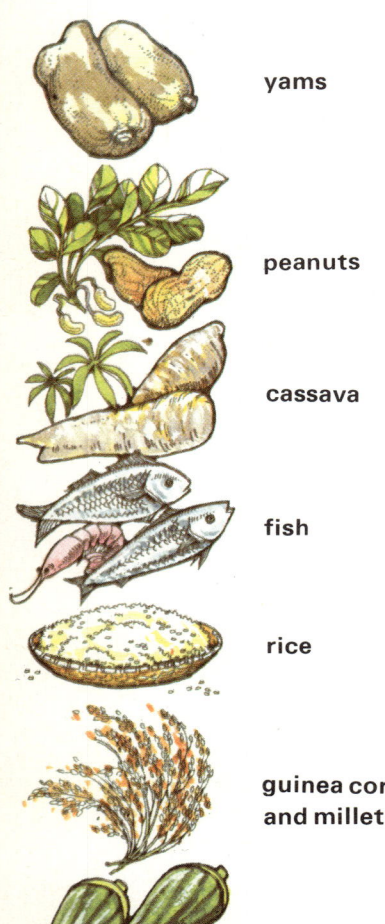

Staple foods in the Nigerian diet

The staple foods are meat and fish cooked with highly flavoured vegetables and spices. They are accompanied by a starchy root or grain.

yams

peanuts

cassava

fish

rice

guinea corn and millet

okra

bananas

palm nuts

The basic diet

Most of the food crops now grown in West Africa came from other parts of the world. Bananas, plantains and yams from Malaysia appeared about 2,000 years ago while maize, cassava and groundnuts were introduced in the last four hundred years.

Regardless of where they came from, these are the main starchy foods now used in cooking, prepared in a variety of forms to accompany hot stews, soups and sauces. Spices are used freely to flavour the rather poor meat and fish available in Nigeria.

What to ask for

Visitors do not normally get a chance to eat Nigerian food unless they are invited to a

GROUNDNUT STEW
2 lb chicken (cut into pieces)
½ lb fresh tomatoes
½ lb onions
½ lb garden eggs (egg-plants or aubergines)
4 oz okra
4 hard boiled eggs
1 pint cooking oil
1 oz tomato paste
½ lb groundnut paste (or peanut butter)
1 teaspoon ground red pepper
Piece of root ginger
1 oz shrimp powder (or shrimps)
3 pints salted water

Nigerian home. Knowing that the English are very attached to their beans, chips and custard, Nigerians are very modest about serving their traditional dishes in restaurants and hotels.

The most interesting dishes come from the south of the country and many of them are similar to those found in other West African countries. When well prepared the most delicious dishes are jollof rice with peppered chicken, palm oil chop, groundnut or palmnut stew, and okro soup.

Nigerian towns and cities are full of cheap 'chop bars' or restaurants where you can get a plain but satisfying meal. The usual Nigerian habit is to eat with the fingers, but forks and spoons are catching on. With their meals Nigerians usually drink water but on social occasions they become serious drinkers. The most famous traditional drink is palm wine, which must be tapped fresh from the tree each morning. Various gins and spirits are also distilled, and Nigerian beer is a potent brew.

Boil chicken for 20 minutes in salted water with a few onion slices and a piece of ginger. Remove the meat from the stock and fry till golden brown. Fry the rest of the onions, tomatoes, shrimps and pepper. Add the groundnut paste diluted with a little water and pour the mixture over the meat. Add more water, adjust seasoning and simmer for about ¾ hour until the meat is tender and the stew is cooked (when oil starts to rise). Prepare and boil separately garden eggs, okra and hard-boiled eggs and add before serving in the traditional black pot. Serve with a dish of plain boiled rice. For groundnut soup, add more water to the stew and serve with fufu (boiled yam, plantain, cassava or coco-yam pounded to a puree in a heavy wooden mortar). Fried slices of plantain, or 'Dodo', are an extra delicacy.

▲ Villagers prepare the day's main meal. In a small village like this each family has its own cooking hut. Depending on the weather and the time of day the food is eaten inside or outdoors.

▶ Sifting grain before the long process of pounding, which in turn makes it suitable for cooking as a kind of porridge to accompany the main meat dish.

▲ Selling fried corn on the street. This is one of a whole range of ready-cooked snacks you can buy on the streets of Nigerian towns and villages. At other stalls you may find meat kebabs, egg sandwiches, roasted peanuts or fried plantains.

▶ A grain store in a Nigerian village, into which a family puts its annual harvest of millet or sorghum grain. It is raised off the ground to protect the contents from damp during the rainy season. The roof is detachable. Grain is put into or taken out of the granary through the hole at the top.

Life set to music

Traditional instruments

▶ A balafon or zylophone. The pods are made of gourd and act as resonators. The size of the gourds is matched to the size and pitch of the wooden bars.

▶ A northern shepherd boy may play a flute while his flock grazes. The tunes are wistful and sad, drifting over the wide open spaces of the Nigerian savannah.

▼ Bowharps and a hand drum. The resonators of these bowharps are hollowed out of wood and covered with skin. The instrument probably originated in Egypt 5,000 years ago.

The importance of rhythm

Rhythm is the dominant element in African music and to create rhythm one needs no instruments at all, just one's feet on the ground, hands on a table or two pieces of wood to knock together. But Nigeria has a wealth of traditional instruments that have been handed down over the centuries and adapted by succeeding generations.

The most important African instruments are the drums—the rhythm instruments. These vary from huge hollowed-out tree trunks that can boom for many miles across the forest to intricately-made hand drums. The Yoruba have very distinctive talking drums, which are played rapidly and alter according to the pressure put on the side strings.

In northern Nigeria ancient instruments are brought out for festivals: long trumpets, reed pipes, one-string fiddles and beautifully resonant xylophones (balafons).

The new styles

The old instruments are dying out as the young people take up electric guitars, saxophones and Western drumkits. But the new African 'pop' music—called 'High-Life'—still has the insistent and infectious rhythm of its origins and is probably the best dance music in the world.

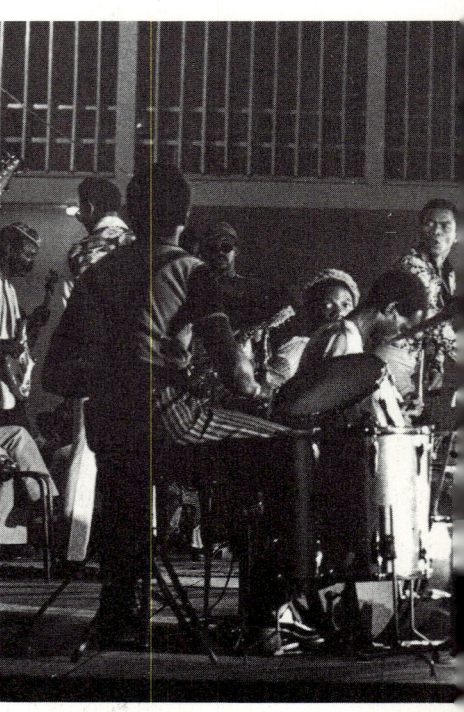

▲ A modern 'Afrobeat' band, starring Fela Ransome-Kuti, one of Nigeria's most innovative musicians. He uses African and Western instruments and composes satirical songs in both Yoruba and pidgin English.

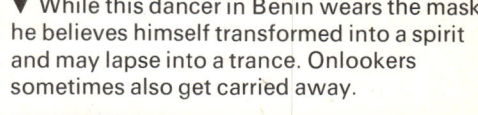
◀ Drummers at an Islamic festival in Kano. The Koran frowns on music in religious worship, but when Islam penetrated into black Africa it had to adjust its dogma.

▼ While this dancer in Benin wears the mask, he believes himself transformed into a spirit and may lapse into a trance. Onlookers sometimes also get carried away.

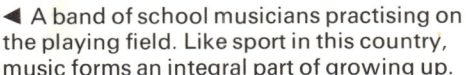
◀ A band of school musicians practising on the playing field. Like sport in this country, music forms an integral part of growing up.

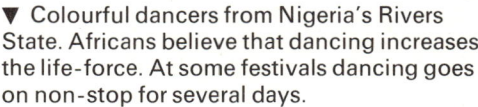
▼ Colourful dancers from Nigeria's Rivers State. Africans believe that dancing increases the life-force. At some festivals dancing goes on non-stop for several days.

Arts and crafts

▲ The dyepits in Kano shown here are as old as the city itself. The workers are descended from a long line of dyers who have been producing ever-changing patterns and designs for centuries, though always in blue. The pits are protected from the sun by basketwork 'hats'.

▼ A Yoruba carved door panel showing a domestic scene. Doors like this have been carved by master craftsmen for the palaces of the Yoruba kings for hundreds of years. This is a more modern work by a carver trained in the old tradition, using typical Yoruba stylization of faces and hairstyles.

Past treasures

Nigeria has rich artistic traditions going back to the earliest inhabitants. The clay heads of Nok represent the beginning of a tradition that flowered at Ife in the twelfth century AD. The Ife bronze heads are of such quality that the first white men to find them could not believe that they were the work of African artists—which they undoubtedly were.

The Benin kingdom also produced some of the finest bronze work in the world, as well as carvings and sculptures in wood and ivory. Benin art is not true 'tribal art', since it served to glorify a royal court rather than the tribal spirits.

Nigeria is unique in having so many art treasures. About nine-tenths of all known African sculpture more than 100 years old is from Nigeria. By good luck these have been well preserved, although it is impossible to determine how much wooden sculpture has perished because of the climate and white ants. But the impermanence of African art provided the source of its infinite variety. When masks rotted away replacements were carved by new artists.

Living crafts

Age-old traditions of craftsmanship survive in the making of everyday practical objects such as baskets, bags, body ornaments, clothes and textiles, sandals, furniture etc.

Perhaps the most interesting crafts centre in Nigeria is the town of Bida, which is the capital of the Nupe people. It produces some unique artifacts, including glass bangles made by a secret method unknown in the rest of Africa.

Weaving, dyeing and printing cloth is an age-old art that still survives in a few parts of Nigeria, especially in Yorubaland and Iboland. The *Akwete* cloth woven in Iboland is particularly prized for its bright colours and imaginative designs. The dyes used to come from tree-bark, leaves and grass, but are now of modern manufacture.

▼ A nation of craftsmen

Some main centres of Nigerian crafts. There are very few areas of the country without some fascinating local arts and traditions. Nigerians are dedicated to their culture and have incorporated much of it into modern industry and trade.

Modern textile factories use locally-designed or popular foreign prints. The colours are always bright. The cloth is cut in lengths which the customer then tailors to his needs.

Traditional architecture, as exemplified by the ancient Habe tower in Katsina, is dying out in the towns, although rural villagers still build their houses with mud and thatch.

▲ A modern mosaic by a Nigerian artist, decorating a wall at the offices of the 'New Nigerian' newspaper in Kaduna. The cyclist is selling copies of the paper, marked 'NN'.

▲ Weavers using traditional looms to make scarf material at Oyo, Western State, one of the main craft centres in Nigeria. Weaving is also practised in the other states of the Federation.

◄ Leather worker at Naraguta near Jos. They turn out their finely worked goods (handbags, belts, pouffes etc) mainly for the tourist market, but are faithful to traditional designs.

Getting around in Nigeria

A Nigeria Airways 707 liner loading on the runway at Kano airport.

On foot and by road

When Nigeria was but a collection of smaller states and kingdoms, travel between its various parts was restricted to trade. This was well developed in the north —which is open country and suitable for camels, horses, and donkeys—but in the thickly forested south all travel was by canoe on the rivers or else on foot, with goods carried on the head.

At the beginning of this century the British started building rough roads, railways and then airports. In Africa good roads are difficult to construct and maintain. In the rainy season an earth road can be completely washed away, with nothing left but a mass of ruts and potholes. Now the Government is spending a great deal of money surfacing the old roads with tarmac and constructing completely new highways between the main centres. As a result Nigeria already has one of the best road systems in Africa. Nigerians have a choice of methods of road travel, according to their means. The slow and cheap way is by 'mammy wagon', a bus which stops every few hundred yards. In addition there are taxis, mini-buses, and comfortable coach services. Each town has a 'motor park' where the passenger can take the vehicle of his choice to his destination.

Trains and planes

Nigerian trains are an amusing relic of the colonial era, still driven by steam and slow enough for the passengers to jump off, buy a loaf of bread and jump on again while they are moving.

Business men and Government officials prefer to fly from main town to main town by *Nigerian Airways* jets which have fairly regular routes all over the country. New air-conditioned hotels are being built in every main town. These tend to be expensive but travellers are often invited to stay with acquaintances along their route. Hospitality is a valued African tradition.

Although travel is becoming more reliable and convenient than it used to be, nobody should be in a hurry in Nigeria. There are always unforeseen delays and breakdowns.

▼ Women and children often carry even heavier loads than this on their heads. This age-old method of transport has certain advantages: it keeps the hands free and gives women a most graceful posture.

▲ Canoes on the river Niger, the original method of river travel. The Niger flows for hundreds of miles through Nigeria and a river trip is one of the most exciting ways of seeing the country.

▲ A typical Lagos 'mammy wagon' — a small truck converted to take passengers on wooden benches. The drivers often paint slogans like 'Save us O Father' or 'Safe journey' to ward off bad luck.

▲ Sahara transport. Despite his reputation for bad temper, the camel is surprisingly tolerant of demanding work. He makes displeasure known, however, by spitting, screaming and lying down on the job.

▶ Boy selling plastic toys on the modern Eko bridge in Lagos. The traffic jams are frequent so these boys make a good living selling newspapers, cigarettes and sweets just by standing at the roadside.

City life— Lagos and Kano

▼ A view over Lagos island, the commercial and administrative centre. On the right is Apapa port and industrial area on the mainland, where the shanty towns are situated. Two road bridges link the island to the mainland. On the seaward side of the island are popular bathing beaches.

Lagos

The population of this capital city has grown from a few thousand at the turn of the century to well over a million in the 1970s—a rapid growth that has not allowed for proper planning, sanitation, water supplies or housing. Now that the Government has more money from the oil industry it is able to spend it on roads, housing estates and reclaiming land from the surrounding lagoons, but the process is a slow one. The inhabitants have to put up with agonising traffic jams at all times of the day, while the miserable conditions of the shanty towns are a health hazard.

But for all this Lagos is a lively and boisterous city with a fascinating history. It dates back to the seventeenth century when a local Yoruba ruler moved onto Lagos island to escape harassment from the Benin kingdom. In 1704 the Portuguese, who gave the city its name, helped the rulers to build a palace in return for exclusive slaving rights. The good harbour made it an important trading centre.

Some historic parts of the city remain, including the original Oba's palace, the old market and the 'Brazilian quarter', with its architecture brought by freed slaves from South America in the mid-1800s.

▲ Lagos street scene. Pedestrians and traffic interweave amid a continuous honking of car horns, while scooters mass along the pavements.

◄ A shanty town on the mainland sector of Lagos. This area has expanded in a haphazard manner as more people leave farming villages for life in the big city.

Kano

The largest of the ancient Hausa cities of the north, Kano is also modern Nigeria's third largest town, after Lagos and Ibadan, and an important industrial area. Around the original walled city the new commercial districts sprawl along tree-lined avenues until they blend with the neighbouring farmlands. The mass of the working population is crammed into the *Sabon Gari* (strangers' district). Kano has many faces, from the medieval atmosphere of the old market to colonial-style sporting clubs and the carefree nightlife of the new Nigeria.

The decorations on some of the houses in Kano have an ancient symbolic meaning. The interiors are more ornate than the outsides and are painted in bright colours.

Founded before 1000AD, Kano had for centuries been a major terminus of the trans-Saharan camel trade. At the Kurmi market in the heart of the old city traders from the Sahara and North Africa still sell their wares alongside the Hausas' stalls of woven and dyed cloth, basketwork, leatherwork and jewellery.

The best way to see the old city is on a bicycle accompanied by a Hausa guide. In this part of Nigeria very few people speak English.

▲ A general view of the old city. The mud-walled houses—common to the towns and cities of this part of Africa—are perfectly suited to the climate. In the heat of the day they remain cool inside; the walls then retain the heat to ward off the chill of the night during the dry season.

▲ A typical street scene in the old city. At the end of each rainy season the mud buildings are resurfaced. If this is not done they decay and collapse.

▶ The huge mud walls of the old city measure 11 miles in circumference and contain 16 gates, the principal one being Kofar Motta. This small gate now opens into a house.

A proud past

▲ This is how a Dutch trader saw Benin in the seventeenth century. The Oba's palace stands apart from the city which was laid out in straight avenues and enclosed by walls.

Diverse cultures

Nigeria groups together peoples whose different histories, cultures and languages reflect the geographical separation between West Africa's savannah and forestlands. What is now the northern part of Nigeria was dominated by the Hausa and Borno emirates, whose history is tied up with the rich medieval empires of the Sahel (the area immediately south of the Sahara). These states were also influenced by the arrival from North Africa of Islam.

In the forests of the southeast, the Ibo, Ibibio and Efik peoples had a much more fragmented society, existing without any formal political system. The only links between different villages came through descent from common ancestors, belief in a common God and use of related dialects.

Between the extremes of the north and the southeast came the Yoruba and Bini (of Benin) people of the southwest, a land of both forest and woodland savannah. The states and kingdoms that developed here spread outwards to influence neighbouring peoples. These were African states whose growth owed nothing to Islam or to Europe, although legend links them to Ancient Egypt.

The Benin Kingdom

Benin began its rise as a prominent African state in the twelfth century AD, when it took its ruling dynasty from the earlier Yoruba kingdom of Ife. The rulers, known as Obas, reigned by hereditary succession and had absolute spiritual, political and military power. Obas were rarely seen in public, appearing only for ceremonial occasions. They fostered one of the most striking and extravagant artistic traditions in Africa.

In the sixteenth century, after the European traders had arrived on the coast, Benin went into a slow decline. In 1897 a British expeditionary force attacked and destroyed the city.

▼ A terracotta head from the 'Nok culture' of 500 BC-AD 200. This Neolithic society is believed to have influenced the cultural growth of Ife, which in turn was the basis of the sophisticated Yoruba civilization.

▲ The present Oba of Benin, Akenzua II, in full regalia. The pink garment is made entirely of coral. The Oba now has a purely ceremonial role, though he still claims descent from earlier 'divine' kings.

▲ A council of elders in a village near Lagos. Elders of the community still decide local affairs and supervize the practise of traditional law.

► A sixteenth century bronze head from Benin, cast at the height of the empire's power and influence.

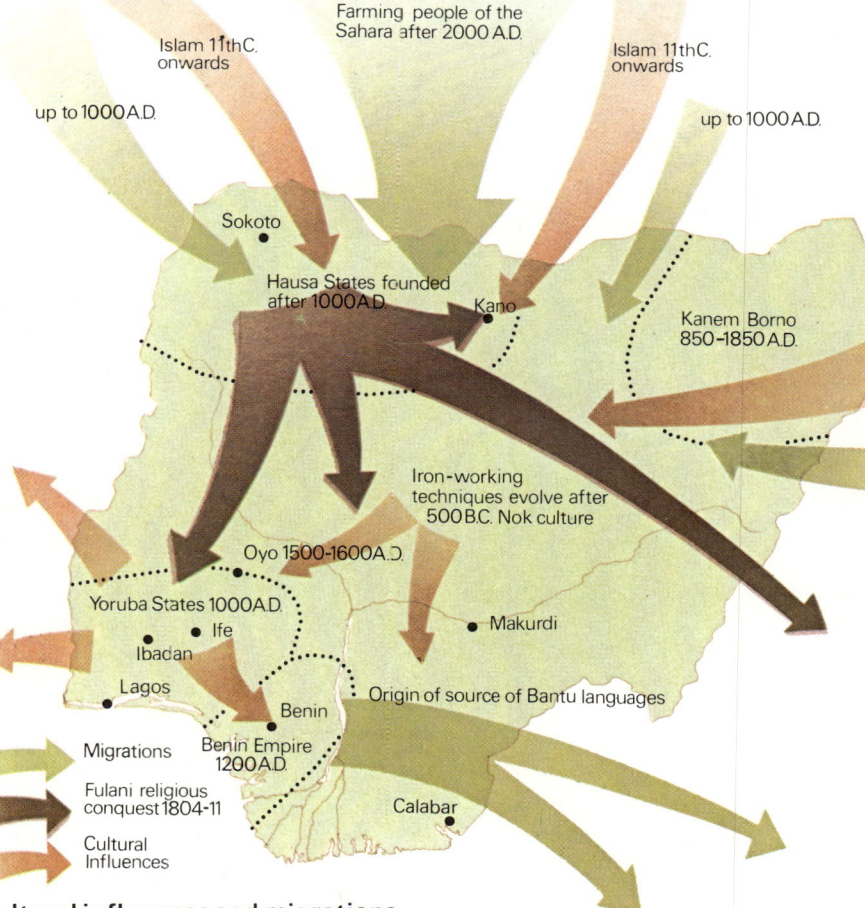

Farming people of the Sahara after 2000 A.D.

Islam 11th C. onwards

Islam 11th C. onwards

up to 1000 A.D.

up to 1000 A.D.

Sokoto

Hausa States founded after 1000 A.D.

Kano

Kanem Borno 850–1850 A.D.

Iron-working techniques evolve after 500 B.C. Nok culture

Oyo 1500–1600 A.D.

Yoruba States 1000 A.D.

Ife

Makurdi

Ibadan

Lagos

Origin of source of Bantu languages

Benin

Migrations

Benin Empire 1200 A.D.

Fulani religious conquest 1804–11

Cultural Influences

Calabar

Cultural influences and migrations

► The main migrations into and out of the area now known as Nigeria came to an end around AD 1000, but the cultural interchange continued. The nineteenth century Fulani conquest was fired by religion.

God, glory and slaves

Principal slave routes

▼ Where African slaves went at the height of trade in the eighteenth century. European traders operated a 'triangular' Atlantic trade: guns, cloth and cheap goods to Africa, slaves to the New World and sugar to Europe.

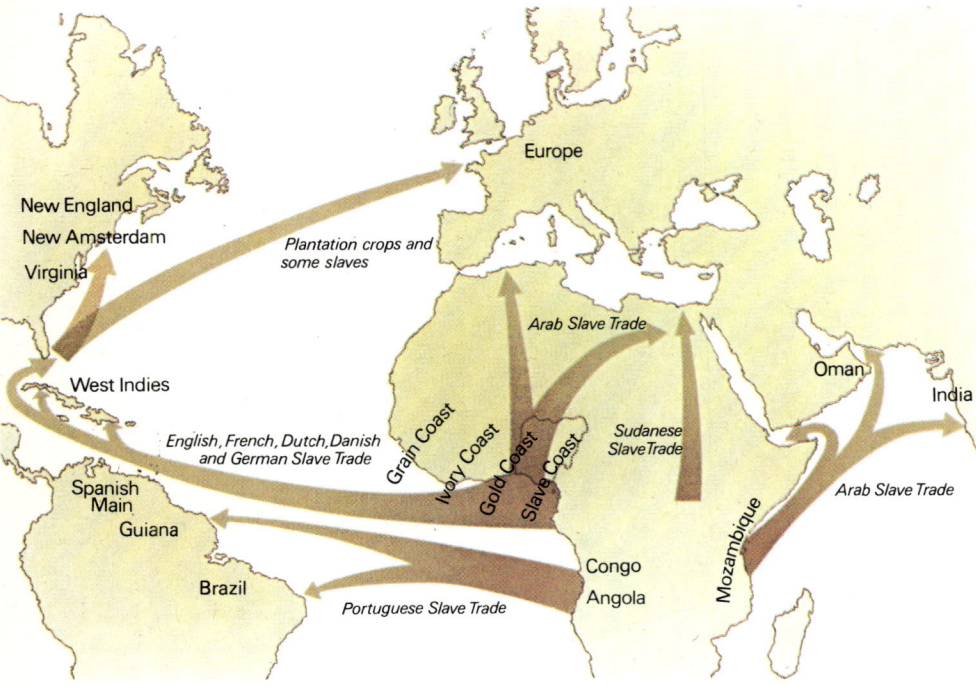

An evil commerce

The first European nation to establish trading posts along the West African coast was Portugal, which opened diplomatic relations with Benin at the end of the fifteenth century. The Portuguese were soon followed by British, Dutch and other traders in search of gold, ivory and spices. But when the new plantations in America and the West Indies were developed in the seventeenth century, the traders began to think of Africa only as a source of slave labour.

Slavery had already existed in Africa, but the Europeans gave the trade a foul and inhuman dimension. Whereas Africans had looked after slaves as members of their own families, the Europeans did not think of slaves as people and their suffering caused them no concern.

The European demand for slaves had the unfortunate effect of turning African tribes against each other. If one kingdom could defeat another in battle it was entitled to seize slaves whom it could then sell at the coast. The Ibo people were the main sufferers from the trade; they were supplied to the coast by the *Aro*, an evil clique of men who controlled the dreaded oracle of the Ibo's supreme deity, *Chukwu*; a man who

▲ A poster advertizing slaves for sale in the West Indies. The callous treatment meted out to African slaves, both on board ship and on the plantations, made them wonder if Europeans were monsters or devils.

▶ The unhappy cargo of a slaver. Olaudah Equiano, a slave who later bought his freedom wrote: 'I was put down under the decks . . . With the loathesomeness of the stench and crying together I became so sick and low that . . . I wished for death to relieve me'.

had been convicted of a crime would be 'swallowed up' by the oracle, i.e. sent into slavery.

Perhaps the most disastrous effect of the slave trade was the heritage of racial hatred it generated. Racialism was originally perpetrated by whites against all other races; miraculously it has not turned Africa away from Europe as much as it might have done. But millions died on the ships and harsh plantations.

Stability destroyed

In Nigeria the slave trade caused internal turbulence that undermined the authority of the old kingdoms, such as Benin and Oyo, a powerful Yoruba state. Mere fishing villages on the coast became wealthy and powerful, while from the north the Fulani waged a Holy War for Islam—almost reaching Ibadan.

When the European powers abolished slavery in the nineteenth century, they sought new types of trade with the West Africans. Explorers set out to discover more about the inland areas and their produce. They were soon followed by traders and missionaries, whose presence paved the way for colonial rule.

▲ Missionaries followed in the footsteps of the explorers and early traders. This old photograph shows the benefits of their medical skills. They also set up the first schools. Their work was mainly confined to the south. They did not try to compete with Islam in the north.

▼ Mungo Park (1771-1806), a Scottish doctor, was determined to follow the course of the Niger to the sea. He set out from Gambia in 1805 and almost certainly reached Bussa, the site of Nigeria's new Kainji Dam, where he was probably killed going over the falls. His diaries were never found.

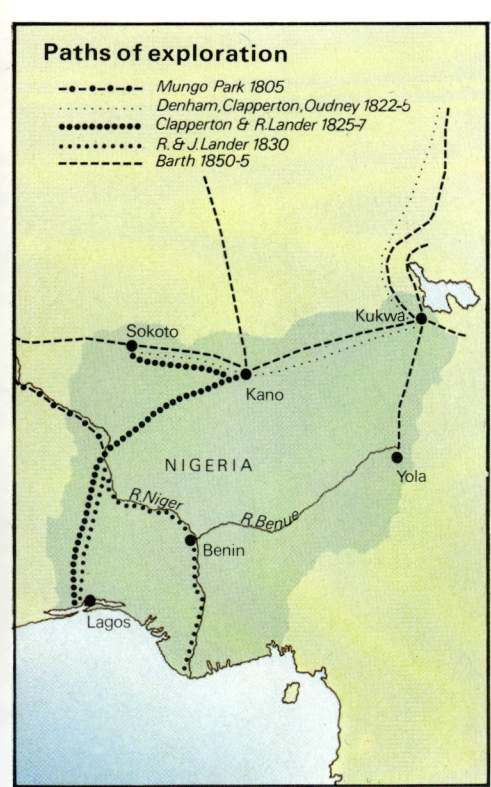

Paths of exploration

- -·-·-·- Mungo Park 1805
- ·········· Denham, Clapperton, Oudney 1822-5
- ●●●●●●●● Clapperton & R. Lander 1825-7
- ▬▬▬▬ R. & J. Lander 1830
- ------ Barth 1850-5

Sokoto
Kukwa
Kano
NIGERIA
Yola
R. Niger
R. Benue
Benin
Lagos

▲ After Mungo Park was killed at Bussa in 1806, the Lander Brothers completed his journey down the Niger in 1830-32. Hugh Clapperton travelled extensively in northern Nigeria and died near Sokoto in 1827. Barth, a German, travelled widely in West Africa.

The march of colonialism

The British advance

Territory under British control C.1880

British Advances after 1884 (with dates)

Colonial frontiers with dates of determination

1898 - 1906
Sokoto 1902
1903
Gwandu
Zaria
Kano
1885
Jos Plateau
Bussa
1906
1894
Ilorin
1885
Ibadan
Lokoja
Benin
British
French
1885

GULF OF GUINEA

ATLANTIC OCEAN

A change of policy

Until the ninteenth century European interest in Africa was confined to the profits to be made from slavery. After years of protest from humanitarians this policy changed dramatically towards the abolition of slavery, and more interest was taken in exploring Africa's interior. In the footsteps of the explorers came missionaries looking for converts and trading companies looking for raw materials like palm oil.

Britain established its supremacy in the Niger delta area in 1852, when steamships started to sail from Liverpool to the trading posts along the coast and up the Niger. In 1861 Britain declared Lagos a colony. A conference of European powers in Berlin in 1885 designated the Niger delta as a British 'sphere of influence'. The Royal Niger Company then made treaties with African rulers, whose areas became a protectorate in 1887. By 1900 the whole of Nigeria was under formal British control.

Lugard's role

Frederick Lugard was Governor of the north between 1900 and 1906, administering through traditional rulers. When he became Governor of all Nigeria in 1912 he imposed the same system on the south. In Iboland he had to create 'chiefs' where none had existed before. The south, however, benefited from British education and social services while the north saw little modernization.

The British-educated elite in the south was the first group to start agitating against colonial rule, but moves towards independence did not start until after World War II, when Dr. Nnamdi Azikiwe formed the first nationalist movement. Britain introduced limited self-rule in 1952.

◄ After taking nominal control of Nigeria in 1900 the British conducted military campaigns against tribes that refused to accept their rule. Troops were recruited locally. It took over ten years to complete the imposition of 'indirect rule' in the north.

▲ The arrival of District Commissioner Ambrose at Ikere Ekiti in Yorubaland in 1895, recorded by a local artist on a Yoruba palace door. Until roads were built and cars introduced the colonial officers and traders were always transported in this grand manner

► The 1902 expedition against the Ibibios. A captive is released on taking an oath to win over villagers who continued to resist the British advance.

▼ Frederick (later Lord) Lugard, as an Army officer, was responsible for many British colonial conquests in Africa. His greatest challenge was as Governor in Nigeria.

► The Western-style marriage ceremony has been enthusiastically adopted by many Christian Nigerians. This is an expensive society wedding in Benin.

▼ A hangover from colonial days in modern Nigeria. Eventually these traces of colonialism will disappear, including the British-style red pillar boxes and traffic signs that are still found in parts of Lagos.

Independence and civil war

An uneasy federation

Even before Nigeria became independent its main problem was rivalry between the three regions: north, west and east. Each was suspected by the other two of wanting to dominate the country.

Independence itself, in October 1960, was peaceful. People looked at Nigeria with admiration for its apparent stability and economic promise, but under the surface was a growing resentment between regional power groups. Politicians began to behave in a ruthless fashion to eliminate opposition and were obviously becoming excessively rich on the proceeds of power.

A military coup in January 1966 eliminated a number of the most powerful and unpopular politicians but put nothing in their place. The northern Hausas suspected that the eastern Ibos were out to dominate them. Ibos living in the north were the victims of ghastly massacres.

In July 1966 northern troops turned on their Ibo comrades and power passed to northern officers under Lt. Col. Yakubu Gowon (who, being a Christian from a minority tribe, could not be identified with the former power blocs of Hausa, Yoruba and Ibo).

The military governor of the east, Lt. Col. Ojukwu, refused to recognise Gowon's authority. East and north were at loggerheads in the army and in the streets. Ibos in the north fled to escape the terrible massacres.

The horror of civil war

After futile attempts to reach agreement, Ojukwu finally took the East from the Federation and called it 'Biafra'. A nightmarish civil war lasted from 1967 to 1970; well over a million people died in the fighting or starved to death. 'Biafra' shrank away until it could survive no longer.

Since 1970 there has been a remarkable reconciliation. Regional rivalry has been eliminated by the creation of 12 States, with more to be set up. The problem now facing the military rulers is when they should hand power back to civilian leaders. The process may take several years.

▲ Dr. Nnamdi Azikiwe, who later became Nigeria's first President, and Princess Alexandra at the Independence celebrations in 1960.

▶ Part of a new campaign in the press. Corruption in Nigeria takes many forms: giving bribes to get jobs and contracts, appointing relatives to jobs, and bribing the police. It will probably never disappear.

▼ A Biafran junior officer being interrogated after capture by Federal forces. Many of the officers of the two sides had been close comrades before the war. When Biafra surrendered there were emotional reunions.

DON'T BE CORRUPT

IF YOU ARE, DON'T BLAME US WHEN WE EXPOSE YOU.

▼ Colonel Ojukwu was the son of one of Nigeria's first millionaires and was himself an astute businessman, soldier and politician. He quickly took command of the secessionist emotions in Eastern Nigeria in 1966 to create his mythical Republic of Biafra. But he failed to give it a firm political basis, or find strong foreign support. Before Biafra surrendered he fled to the Ivory Coast.

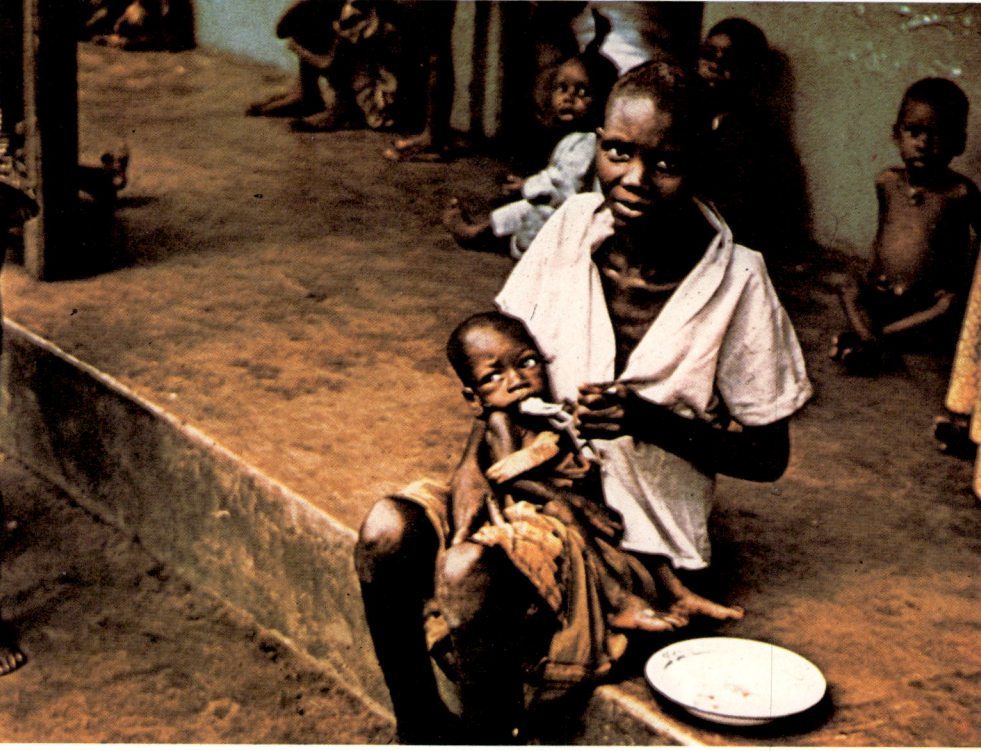

▲ Children were the greatest sufferers from widespread malnutrition in the southeast when the Ibo population clung together in the fading hope of successfully establishing 'Biafra'. Many refugees were continuously on the move to avoid the fighting. Finally they returned to their homes to find a greater chance of prosperity in one Nigeria.

The new Nigeria

Gowon created the 12 states in 1967. They have been the basic formula for stability since the secession in the East was suppressed.

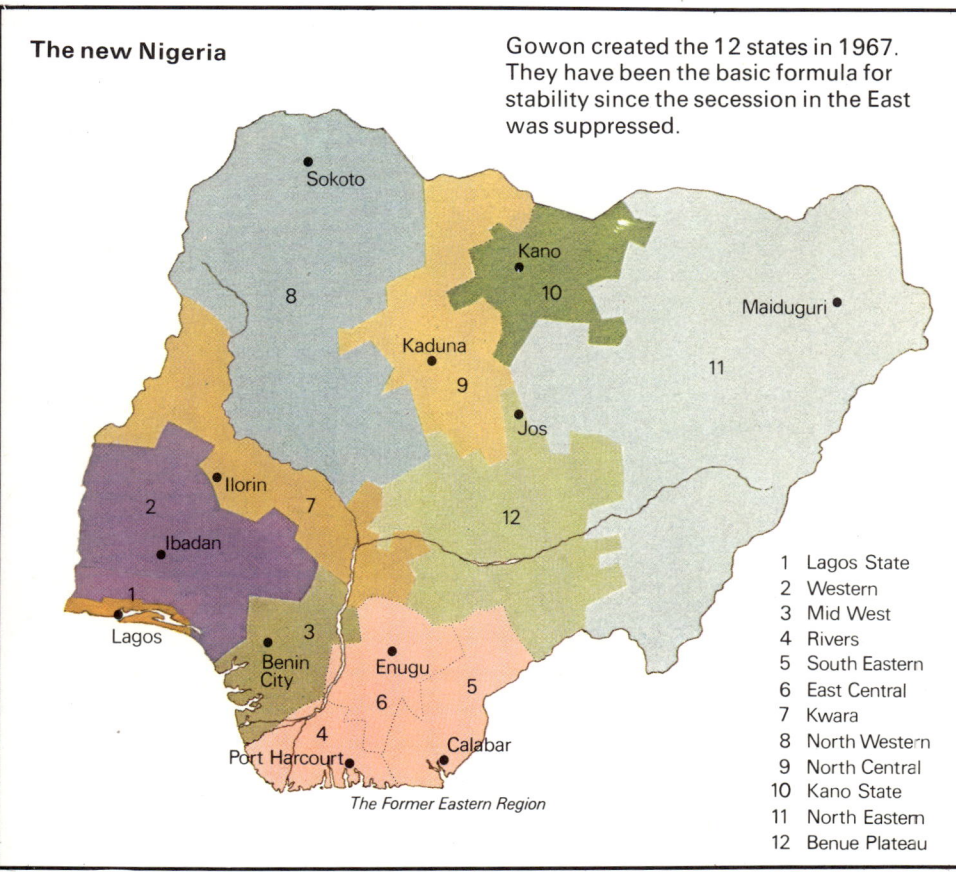

Sokoto

Kano

10

Maiduguri

8

Kaduna

9

11

Jos

Ilorin

7

2

12

Ibadan

1

Lagos

3

Enugu

Benin City

5

6

4

Calabar

Port Harcourt

The Former Eastern Region

1 Lagos State
2 Western
3 Mid West
4 Rivers
5 South Eastern
6 East Central
7 Kwara
8 North Western
9 North Central
10 Kano State
11 North Eastern
12 Benue Plateau

▲ In the 1966 crisis Lieutenant Colonel Gowon (now General) emerged as the most capable leader to represent the whole country. He comes from a small tribe in the Benue-Plateau State. He has a reputation for personal honesty and is admired for his spirit of forgiveness after the Civil War. Recently he was Chairman of the Organization of African Unity for a year.

Heroes in fact and fiction

Crafty creatures

In fiction

In African fables the heroes are often animals of the forest who manifest human characteristics. Clever creatures like the spider always manage to outwit the strong and powerful lion and elephant, while the slow and ponderous tortoise makes up for his disadvantages by using his powers of observation to get the better of the hare, the snake, and the boar. The little mouse too escapes from trouble by remaining inconspicuous.

And in fact

Nigeria has many real-life heroes, dating from the distant past up to the present. The kings of the old empires of Borno and Benin are still recalled by their descendant peoples. The fifteenth century King Ewuare of Benin is remembered for his successful conquests and for his city planning.

Nigerians have good reason to honour men who resisted colonialism, from the rulers of nineteenth century coastal states —with names like Jaja, Nana and Pepple— to recent nationalists like Dr. Nnamdi Azikiwe.

▲ Some peoples have their own sacred animals. The Tiv, for example, have a legend that a green tree snake helped their ancestors to cross a river while they were fleeing from their enemies. It formed a bridge for them and then drowned their pursuers. The particular species of snake is still called *ikarem* which means 'my friend'.

In Yoruba folklore, the tortoise is 'the thinker' who outdistances the hare through craft and perseverance. To the Tiv, however, the hare is an unbeatable opponent.

In Hausa stories 'Spider' is the wily trickster who confuses all the other animals, while Dan Katsina and Dan Kano are two rogues who carry out a battle of wits.

▶ Before colonial times the story-teller used to be a central figure in village life, revered for his ability to record and retell history and legends. He reflected the beliefs and social attitudes of the village and was responsible for passing them on to the younger generation. In his tales he would sing, tell jokes and act out all the parts in a realistic manner. The tradition is still very strong.

Tale-bearers

▼ Sir Abubakar Tafawa Balewa, Nigeria's first Prime Minister, assassinated in January 1966. He was a fatherly and respected leader, though the corruption of his Government colleagues brought his downfall.

▼ Brigadier Benjamin Adekunle, far left, the 'Black Scorpion', was Nigeria's most spectacular military campaign leader during the Civil War. His successes and foibles were eagerly reported by the world press.

▲ Dr. Kwame Nkrumah, Ghana's first president, is still remembered in Nigeria as the first African leader to bring his country to independence (in 1957) and for his passionate belief in African unity.

▲ Nigeria's best-known writer, Wole Soyinka, has published plays, poems and novels, and done much to teach the outside world about Nigeria's way of life and culture. But his books are also of universal interest.

The Nigerian character

Old virtues

The first characteristic visitors notice about Nigerians is their enormous friendliness and generosity. In traditional society hospitality to strangers was very highly valued, and this is still the case. Nigerians are also brimming over with good humour. Nothing relieves tension like a good laugh.

Amid the turmoil and bustle of life in modern Nigeria there is still security for everyone in the family. Family solidarity does, however, bolster tribalism, which is the bane of Nigeria's political development.

The easy-going atmosphere of the country is a by-product of the hot climate, which means that nothing works very efficiently. Individual Nigerians are nevertheless very go-ahead and keen to improve their standard of education and knowledge of the world.

Modern vices

Nigerians value success, especially in business and politics. The popular ambition is to become a 'big man' with influence. The

▲ It is said that in applying for a job *who* you know is more important than *what* you know. But technical qualifications are taken very seriously nowadays too.

▲ Nigerians have an inferiority complex about their own products. They prefer to pay more for something imported even if there is no difference in quality.

▲ An argument in the street quickly flares up into a public incident and general free-for-all. The crowd likes to act as judge of skill in arguing.

◄ Modesty is not an attribute that Nigerians appreciate. If they are wealthy they see no reason why they should not display it for the world to see.

'big men' show off their virility by driving fast cars, smoking expensive cigarettes and wearing the latest fashions. Nigerian women too are prone to covet what is expensive, desiring more than anything to be able to wear imported lace cloth, which can cost up to £10 a yard. Some men are driven to succeed merely to satisfy the demands of their rapacious wives and girlfriends.

A successful man still has headaches. Tradition requires him to spread his wealth among his family. He may even find himself responsible for the education of a whole village, including paying for a school building.

The majority of Nigerians are poor and far too busy fending for their families on low wages to have such ambitions. They console themselves with the thought that money only brings unhappiness.

Africans are often accused of laziness. In fact they are capable of tremendously hard work when the need arises but regard it as more important to enjoy life.

▲ Leisure time in Zaria's market-place. Card and board games are played earnestly, with short breaks for work in between, while onlookers place bets with each other. But competition is friendly, if stiff.

▼ Successful city-dwellers are duty-bound to look after their less fortunate country cousins who turn up in the hope of accommodation and a job. It can cause family strain.

▲ Children learn to dance at an early age. The simple village life gives country people a special grace and dignity, which is beginning to disappear in the towns.

A nation on the move

A new nation

The change from a disorganised collection of kingdoms and states to a modern nation in the space of 70 years has been challenging, exciting and at times hair-raising, but Nigeria has a large number of concerned and responsible potential leaders to steer it through its future development.

Politically, Nigeria is still trying to find the perfect recipe for stability among its disparate peoples. The 12-State system, which has worked fairly well since the civil war of 1967-70, may soon be revised to give more areas a chance to be self-governing and to prepare for civilian rule in place of military Government.

Problems of development

The country is developing economically at a breakneck pace. The massive revenues from oil have enabled the Government to spend more than ever before on education, health and communications. Despite this progress there is still a wide gap between income groups. Industrial workers and farmers earn very little.

Agriculture has declined, partly because young people with a little education are unwilling to work in the fields like their fathers. As they leave the countryside the cities are becoming unmanageably overcrowded, and there are not enough jobs.

The biggest economic expansion is in industry. Both foreign and Nigerian companies are setting up new factories all over the country. Some massive projects are proposed, including an iron and steel industry and more oil refineries.

The economy used to be dominated by foreign companies, but in 1974 the Government decreed that in most businesses Nigerians should hold a majority of the shares, so that the profits should remain in Nigeria. Thus, the great natural wealth of Nigeria is, at the moment, exploited for the benefit of its citizens. If the West African giant can continue to direct a just use of its resources, and avoid the pit-falls of a monopolistic and class-ridden society, then the future of Nigeria—and the whole of Africa—must seem the brighter.

▲ Tourists on a beach near Lagos. Few tour operators provide regular services to Nigeria but when its assets are discovered there will be many more visitors.

▼ The first vehicle to be completely designed and built in Nigeria. There are already assembly plants for European cars and soon other modern industries will follow.

▲ General Gowon reconciled with President Nyerere of Tanzania, 1970. Ex-Emperor Haile Selassie of Ethiopia stands centre. Tanzania was one of four African countries that recognised Biafra as a separate nation. Since then, Nigeria has been a force for peace in the whole of Africa.

▼ Nigerian men fear women's liberation will mean that they have to do more domestic work. At the moment few men would be seen dead cooking or washing dishes, except as servants for Europeans, 'big men' or hotels.

▲ Forest cleared for agricultural purposes. There is a danger of a wood shortage and erosion if too much forest is cleared, so elsewhere there are reforestation projects.

▼ An oil rig at Ughelli in the Niger delta area. Much of the oil is drilled offshore. Nigeria now has a majority share in all the drilling operations in the country.

Reference
Human and physical geography

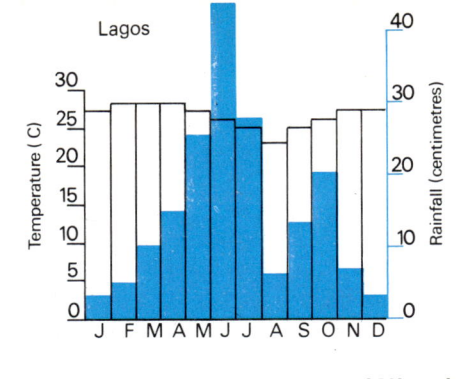

Lagos

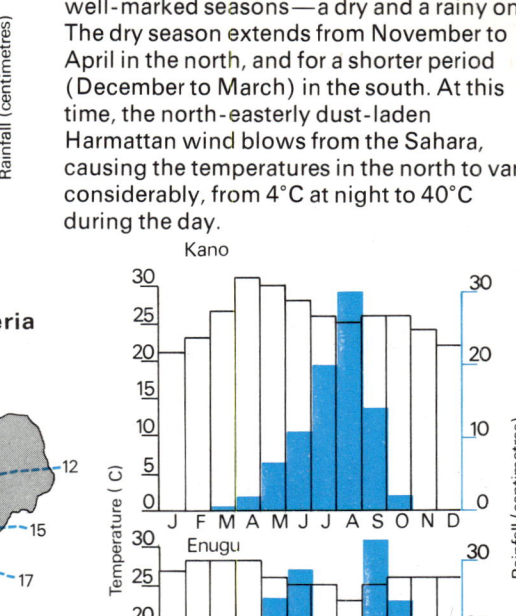

Kano

Enugu

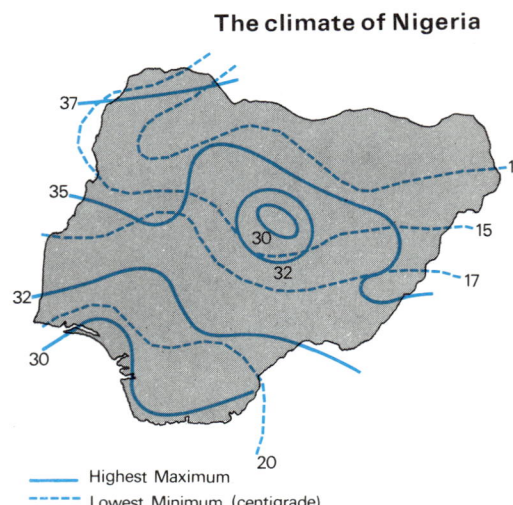

The climate of Nigeria

— Highest Maximum

- - - Lowest Minimum (centigrade)

Nigeria has a number of climatic zones, according to altitude and distance from the sea, but generally speaking there are two well-marked seasons—a dry and a rainy one. The dry season extends from November to April in the north, and for a shorter period (December to March) in the south. At this time, the north-easterly dust-laden Harmattan wind blows from the Sahara, causing the temperatures in the north to vary considerably, from 4°C at night to 40°C during the day.

THE LAND AND PEOPLE

Full title: The Federal Republic of Nigeria.

Position: The Federal Republic of Nigeria is situated on the West Coast of Africa between latitudes 4°20′ and 13°49′ north and longitudes 2°55′ and 14°35′ east. It is bordered to the west by Dahomey, to the north by Niger, to the northeast by Chad, to the east by Cameroon and to the south by the Gulf of Guinea.

Area: The total area is 356,669 square miles (924,000 sq. km.)

Capital: Lagos (population of Lagos State (1973): 2,470,000).

Population: Provisional figures of the 1973 census give a total population of 79,760,000. Nigeria is the most highly populated country in Africa.

Ethnic Groups: Among the 250 distinct ethnic groups in Nigeria the predominant peoples are: in the north the Hausa, Fulani, Tiv, Kanuri, Igala, Idoma, Igbirra and Nupe; in the southwest the Yoruba, Edo, Urhobo, Itsekiri and Ijaw; and in the southeast the Ibo, Ibibio, Efik, Ekoi and Ijaw.

Languages: English is the official language and is widely used but the following Nigerian languages predominate in their areas of origin, each with its own literature: Hausa in the north; Yoruba and Edo in the southwest; Ibo and Efik in the southeast.

Religion: Islam is predominant in the north and also has followers in the southwest, although Christianity is the main religion in the south (divided between Catholics, Protestants, Methodists and Presbyterians). Throughout Nigeria are peoples who still practise traditional religions.

Head of State: General Yakubu Gowon.

Armed forces: 157,000 members of the army, navy and air force; 100,000 reserves.

External Relations: Nigeria is a member of the United Nations and many of its agencies, the Organization of African Unity and the Commonwealth. It co-operates with neighbouring countries in the West African Economic Community, the Niger River Commission, the Chad Basin Commission and the West African Rice Development Association. In 1971, Nigeria joined the Organization of Petroleum Exporting Countries.

The natural vegetation of Nigeria

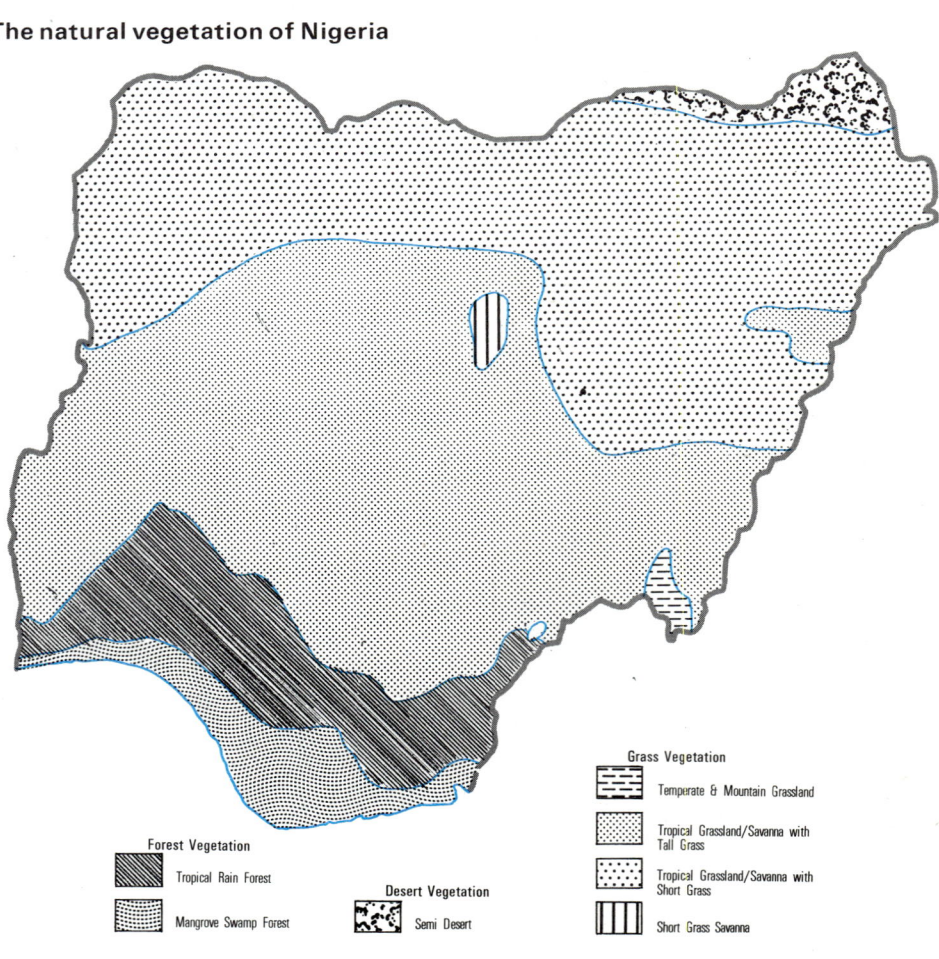

Forest Vegetation

▨ Tropical Rain Forest

▦ Mangrove Swamp Forest

Desert Vegetation

▨ Semi Desert

Grass Vegetation

▤ Temperate & Mountain Grassland

⣿ Tropical Grassland/Savanna with Tall Grass

⣀ Tropical Grassland/Savanna with Short Grass

▥ Short Grass Savanna

Population density

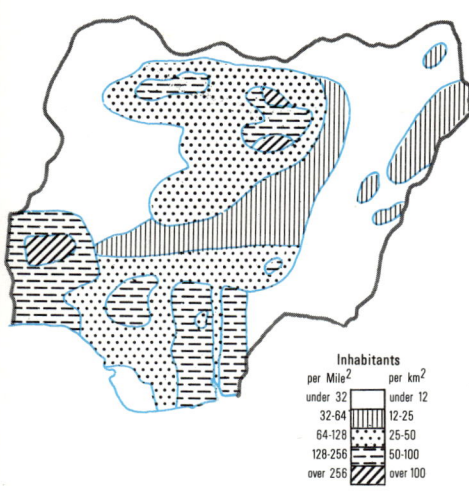

Inhabitants
per Mile²	per km²
under 32	under 12
32-64	12-25
64-128	25-50
128-256	50-100
over 256	over 100

Distribution of inhabitants

If, as the provisional results of the 1973 census would suggest, Nigeria's population is over 79 million, it is the eighth most populous country in the world, coming after Brazil. Previous censuses gave Nigeria a population of 56 million in 1963 and of 30 million in 1953.

The six northern States, with 51 million in 1973, have almost two-thirds of the total. The six southern States have 28 million people. While the population of Lagos State grew considerably in the previous ten years, as is natural for the Federation's capital, that of Western State appears to have fallen from 9.5 million to 8.9 million. Even more unpredictable was the gigantic 100% rise in the populations of Kano and North-Eastern States over the ten-year period to 1973.

Generally speaking, the population is unevenly distributed, with the main concentrations being in the urbanised southwest (the Lagos and Ibadan areas), in the intensely populated countryside of the southeast and in the urban areas of the north (Kano, Zaria etc).

Population of principal towns

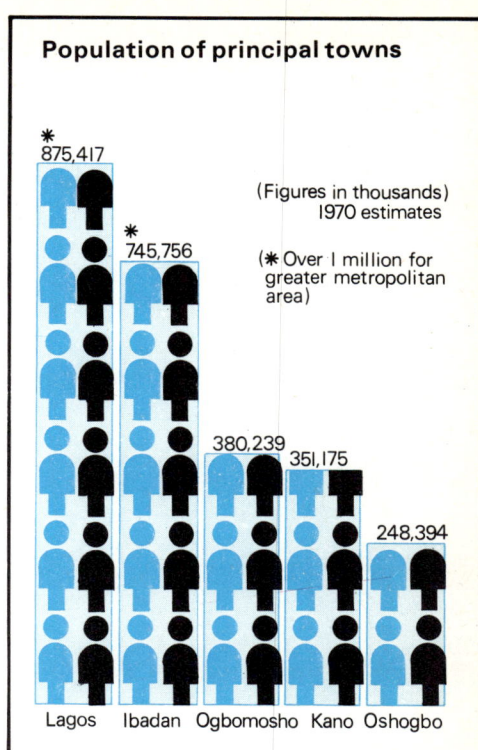

(Figures in thousands) 1970 estimates

(✳ Over I million for greater metropolitan area)

✳ 875,417 — Lagos
✳ 745,756 — Ibadan
380,239 — Ogbomosho
351,175 — Kano
248,394 — Oshogbo

Government

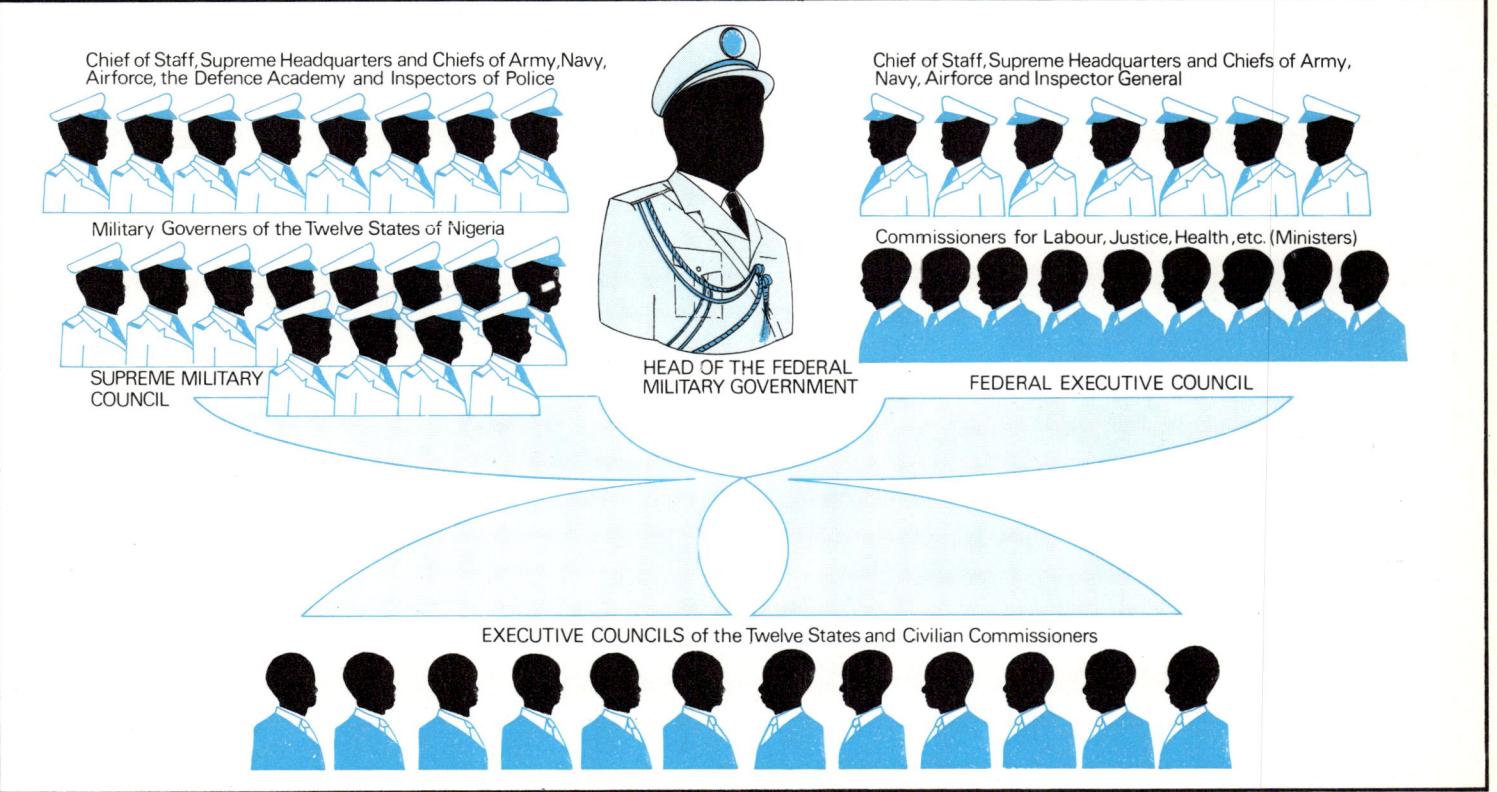

Chief of Staff, Supreme Headquarters and Chiefs of Army, Navy, Airforce, the Defence Academy and Inspectors of Police

Military Governers of the Twelve States of Nigeria

SUPREME MILITARY COUNCIL

HEAD OF THE FEDERAL MILITARY GOVERNMENT

Chief of Staff, Supreme Headquarters and Chiefs of Army, Navy, Airforce and Inspector General

Commissioners for Labour, Justice, Health, etc. (Ministers)

FEDERAL EXECUTIVE COUNCIL

EXECUTIVE COUNCILS of the Twelve States and Civilian Commissioners

The Supreme Military Council has been the principal source of power in Nigeria since the coup d'etat of July 1966. Its chairman is automatically the Head of State who in turn presides over the Government of the Federal Republic. This Government consists of both military men and civilians and is responsible for the day-to-day running of the country, with Commissioners (or Ministers) responsible for sectors such as Finance, Foreign Affairs, Economic Development, Education, Information etc. Most of these jobs are duplicated at the level of the twelve States. It is not always clear where the authority of the Federal Commissioners ends and that of the State Commissioners begins.

The legal system is based on English law. There is a Federal Supreme Court, presided over by the Chief Justice, which is the final court of appeal. It has power to interpret the Constitution and hears disputes over legal rights between State Governments, or between a State and the Federal Government. Each State has a High Court.

Reference
History

56

Main Events in Nigerian History

B.C.

before 2500 The original Old Stone Age peoples break up into numerous smaller groups.
The Sahara begins to dry up.

2000-1000 Farming peoples move southwards out of the Sahara.

500 Farming develops in the forest areas.
Iron working evolves on the Jos Plateau. The birth of the Nok culture.

100 Camels introduced from Asia for the Trans-Saharan trade, in place of horses, donkeys and chariots.

A.D.

300 Iron working spreads.
Population migrations into Nigeria from north and east and out of Nigeria to the southeast

850 Kanem empire founded around Lake Chad.

1000 First Hausa and Yoruba states established.

1086 Kanem emperor Ibn Abd al-Jelil accepts Islam.

1100 Ife becomes the main centre of Yoruba culture.

1200 Benin State rises under the Ogiso dynasty.

1300 Ife reaches the height of its influence.

1375 Bulala peoples weaken the Kanem empire.

1400 Nupe state established between Hausa and Yoruba spheres of influence.
Hausa and Yoruba states increase in wealth and power.
Benin increases its territory.

1456 Islam penetrates Hausaland as far as Zaria.

1472 Portuguese visit Benin.

1507 Mai Idris Katakarmabe becomes king of Borno and controls Kanem.

1517 King of Kebbi attacks Gobir and Katsina.

16th century European traders establish relations with coastal states.
Songhai empire invades Hausaland.
Sahara trade at its height.

1553 English visit Benin.

1575 Hausa states revolt against Songhai.

1580-1617 Mai Idris Alooma strengthens Kanem-Borno, which becomes the most powerful state in the region.

17th century Rise of the Yoruba state of Oyo, which extends its power into Dahomey.
New city states emerge in the Niger delta.
Sahara trade less important than Atlantic trade.

1677-81 Kanem-Borno begins to decline once again.

1670-1703 Tuareg and Jukun peoples raid the north.

18th century The slave trade across the Atlantic reaches its height.
The Niger Delta city states become prosperous.
Oyo remains powerful but Benin declines.
Five city states dominate the Niger Delta: Itsekiri in the west, Brass, Elem Kalabari and Grand Bonny to the east, and Calabar at the mouth of the Cross and Calabar rivers.

1804-11 Fulani conquest of Hausaland. Uthman dan Fodio wages a holy war. Caliphate of Sokoto established.

1808 Fulani conquer Kanem-Borno which then rallies under al-Kanemi to repel them.

1817 Revolt in Oyo which is exploited by the Fulani to extend their influence.
Dan Fodio dies.

1830 The Lander brothers sail down the Niger to the sea.

1843 The holy war among the Yoruba is halted at Ibadan.

1846 Civil war in Borno.

1807-56 Slave trade in the Niger Delta changes to palm oil and general commerce.

1856-86 British companies enter the palm oil trade, opening trading posts inland.

1861-2 Lagos ceded to the British crown as a colony.

1860-65 War between Ibadan and other Yoruba states.

1877-93 Ibadan again at war with her neighbours, but conquers them with British help.

1885 Berlin Conference recognises Niger area as a British 'sphere of influence'. Oil Rivers Protectorate declared from Lagos to Calabar.

1886 Royal Niger Company formed as principal agent of British influence, signing treaties with chiefs, etc.

1900 Administrative powers of Royal Niger Company taken over by the Crown. Protectorates of Southern and Northern Nigeria formed, with Lord Lugard as Governor of the North.

1912-14 Lugard becomes Governor-General of both Protectorates, which are then amalgamated.

1922 Legislative Council set up in the south with seats for four elected representatives.

1946 Central Legislature created to represent all Nigeria, with three regional councils. Executive power still in British hands.

1957 Internal Self-Government for East and West Regions.

1959 Internal Self-Government for North.

1960 Independence.

1963 Mid-West Region created.
Nigeria becomes a Republic.

1964-65 Controversy and disturbances over census results and conduct of elections.

1966 Military coup in January. Some top politicians killed. Regions abolished.
Massacre of Ibos in the North, causing extreme bitterness in the East.
Second coup in July. Lt.-Col. Gowon becomes Supreme Commander, re-establishing Federation, but not recognised by the Eastern Military Governor, Lt.-Col. Ojukwu.

1967 Gowon announces creation of 12 States, whereupon Ojukwu declares former Eastern Region to be 'Republic of Biafra'.
Fighting breaks out in July.

1968-69 Federal offensive initially successful but the small Biafran enclave holds out, despite starvation and disease.

1970 Secessionist officers surrender in January.
In October Gowon announces a nine-point programme for the military Government, to be completed by 1976.

1974 Gowon postpones civilian rule.

The inside story
Nigerian writers on their own history include Olaudah Equiano (1745-97), a freed Ibo slave, who wrote an account of his own background and experiences now published as *Equiano's Travels*. Jacob Egharevba wrote *A Short History of Benin*.

The foreign eye
Foreign explorers, travellers and residents in Nigeria have often been inspired to write about their experiences. The best English novels about Nigeria are those written by Joyce Cary, especially *Mister Johnson* and *Aissa Saved*, both written in the 1930s.

The political view
Nigerian politicians whose writings have been published include Obafemi Awolowo, Nnamdi Azikiwe, Sir Abubakar Tafawa Balewa, Sir Ahmadu Bello and Tai Solarin.

The Arts

LITERATURE

Traditional 'literature' was not written but handed down by word of mouth. Only since the 1950s has a written Nigerian literature evolved, mainly in English but with some important works in local languages. At the same time many traditional stories have been collected into anthologies.

The following are among the living Nigerian writers who are producing a distinctive and exciting literature for their country:

Achebe, Chinua
Nigeria's foremost novelist. His works have covered social change from early colonial days to Iboland to the era of corrupt politicians in the 1960s. The best-known novels are *Things Fall Apart* (1958), *No Longer at Ease* (1960), *Arrow of God* (1964) and *A Man of The People* (1966). The Civil War is reflected in his book of short stories, *Girls at War*. His poems have also been published under the title *Beware Soul Brother*.

Aluko, Timothy
A well-known novelist whose favourite subject has been the conflict between old and new in Yoruba society: *One Man, One Wife* (1959), *One Man, One Matchet* (1964), *Kinsman and Foreman* (1966).

Amadi, Elechi
A novelist from the Rivers State who has been in his time a teacher, army officer and top civil servant. *The Concubine* was published in 1966. He is best known for his personal account of the Civil War, *Sunset in Biafra*.

Clark, John Pepper
A poet and playwright whose best-known work is also about the Civil War, a book of poems entitled *Casualties*.

Egbuna, Obi
A playwright and novelist who became well known in Britain for his outspoken views, until he returned embittered to Nigeria in 1971. His best play is *The Anthill* (1965).

Ekwensi, Cyprian
A novelist from the north who is now regarded as one of the father figures of Nigerian literature. His *People of the City*, which deals with the seamy side of Lagos life, was published in 1954. Since then he has written *Jagua Nana, Burning Grass: a Story of the Fulani* and *Beautiful Feathers*.

Ladipo, Duro
Author of *Three Yoruba Plays*. An English adaptation has been published.

Nwapa, Florence
Nigeria's foremost woman writer. Her best-known novel, *Efuru*, is about women in Ibo society.

Nzekwu, Onuora
A novelist who concentrates on the dominant Nigerian theme of cultural conflict: *Wand of Noble Wood* (1961), *Blade Among the Boys* (1962) and *Highlife for Lizards* (1965).

Okara, Gabriel
A poet turned novelist who tried in *The Voice* (1964) to put into English the rhythms of the Ijaw language. The result is a striking poetic novel which pays little regard to conventional English grammar.

Okigbo, Christopher
A poet and novelist killed in the first fighting of the Civil War in 1967. *Heavensgate* (1962), *Limits* (1964).

Omotoso, Kole
Author of *The Combat*, an extended parable of the Nigerian situation during the Civil War.

Rotimi, Ola
A playwright and theatre director attached to the University of Ife: *The Gods Are Not to Blame, Kurunmi*, and *Overrawmin*.

Soyinka, Wole
Nigeria's most famous writer, with an impressive output of plays, poems and novels. His early plays are: *The Swamp Dwellers, The Trials of Brother Jero, A Dance of the Forests, The Lion and the Jewel, The Road* and *Kongi's Harvest. The Interpreters* was his first novel. A collection of poems is entitled *Idanre and other poems*. Soyinka's experience at the hands of the Federal authorities during the Civil War inspired his War Quartet: *Madmen and Specialists* (a play), *A Shuttle in the Crypt* (a collection of poems), *The Man Died* (diaries kept in prison) and *Season of Anomy* (a novel based on the War). He now edits *Transition*, a magazine based in Ghana.

Tutuola, Amos
Tutuola's *The Palm-Wine Drinkard,* (sic) published in 1952, was the first Nigerian novel to be acclaimed overseas. Dylan Thomas described it as "bewitching" and a "tall devilish story". It is based in part on traditional Yoruba stories, embellished by the effects of alcohol. His other books include *My Life in the Bush of Ghosts* and *Feather Woman of the Jungle*.

FINE ART

For centuries Nigerians have been prolific artists in sculpture, carving, engraving and decoration, as well as in music, dancing and singing. For the most part the physical medium of expression has been wood, with the result that few objects can survive more than a generation. The climate and the white ants quickly destroy wood that is not preserved by modern methods. This process is tragic for our knowledge of past artistic styles among the people who did not use bronze, brass or iron. At the same time perishable works of art meant that artistic traditions were always revitalized. New artists were required by the community in each generation; in this way new ideas were being constantly infused.

Despite the loss of many valuable works of art through decay and old age, Nigeria is the source of about nine-tenths of the known works of African sculpture over 100 years old. Even now more and more ancient pieces are being discovered. In the words of William Fagg, an eminent art historian: "It is to Nigeria that all the African nations must look as the principal trustee of the more durable fruits of the Negro artistic genius".

Early Cultures

Nok (c.500 BC-AD 200)
This culture was first discovered in the 1940s by tin miners on the Jos Plateau, who uncovered a number of terracotta heads and small figures of fine workmanship. Since then research over an area of 300 miles, east to west, and 200 miles, north to south, has revealed many more similar figures dating from the same period. The Nok culture is truly African, in that the figures representing humans display the 'African proportion' that still persists as a strong theme in ethnic art (the head takes up one-third or one-quarter of the total height, instead of the true proportion of one-sixth or one-seventh).

Ife (c. AD 800-AD 1300)
The growth of Ife culture corresponded to the development of the Yoruba kingdoms in southwest Nigeria. It is thought that some Ife artistic techniques evolved from the earlier Nok art. Ife art was, however, more naturalistic than any comparable African tradition and also more inventive, especially in the use of bronze.

Even now the Yoruba area is more prolific artistically than any other region of Africa (if not the world). The richness of this people's art is derived from the complexity of their traditional religion.

Benin (c.1300-1700)
During this classical age of Benin art the royal court employed artists versed in Yoruba skills and techniques until a distinctive Benin style emerged. The output was enormous: bronze figures, heads, plaques, masks and altars; ivory heads, amulets, gongs, trumpets and other decorations; and countless wooden pieces which have inevitably disappeared.

Art experts have been able to identify individual masters, whose work displays particular expertise and talent, e.g.: The Master of the Circled Cross, The Master of the Leopard Hunt, The Master of the Engraved Helmets, The Master of the Slit Gongs, The Master of the Cow Sacrifices.

By the eighteenth and nineteenth centuries the tradition had degenerated to one of uninspired imitation. In this it differed from the always lively tribal art beyond the city walls. The classical pieces were however stored in the royal palace until the British Expedition of 1897, when most works of value were shipped to Britain, where they remain today.

Reference
The Economy

FACTS AND FIGURES

Total wealth *(1973)*: 5,780 million naira.

Economic growth rate: About 9 per cent per year.

Main sources of income:

Agriculture: Cocoa, groundnuts, cotton, palm kernels, palm oil, rubber, timber. Food crops for local consumption include millet, maize, sorghum, cassava, sweet potatoes and yams.

Mining: Petroleum, tin, columbite, coal and limestone.

Industry: Textiles, food processing, metal products, drinks, vegetable oil milling, chemicals, petroleum products, cigarettes, clothing, rubber, cement, shoes, matches.

Main trading partners: Great Britain, USA, France, Netherlands, West Germany, Japan, Italy.

Currency: The Naira. £1 sterling = approx. 1.5 naira.

Currency in circulation *(1973)*: 490 million naira.

Balance of payments surplus *(1973)*: 165 million naira.

External assets 1973: 438 million naira.

Energy consumption: petroleum 70%, hydro-electricity 16%, natural gas 9%, coal 5%.

Consumer price index 1973: *(1960=100)*: 190.

Agriculture in Nigeria

Rice · Sugar Cane · Cocoa · Groundnuts · Cotton · Soybeans · Cattle · Copra/Palm Products · Kola · Benniseed · Sheep · Rubber & Timber · Millet · Ginger · Northern & Southern Limits of Yam Growing · Citrus Fruits

Economic growth

Since the mid-1960s petroleum has played a dominant role in Nigeria's economic growth and activity. Production has continued to increase and is now well over two million barrels of crude petroleum a day, making Nigeria Africa's biggest producer. Total crude oil exports are around 100 million metric tons a year.

With the 1974 increases in petroleum prices, Nigeria's national wealth more than doubled. The Government's revenue from oil alone is now well over 2,000 million naira a year. This new-found wealth has enabled the Government to spend lavishly on national development schemes.

In the long term Nigeria cannot rely on its petroleum reserves and there is concern that not enough is being done to increase agricultural production. Crops in the north of the country have suffered from drought but there are plans to step up output of wheat, rice and cotton.

Many light industries have been established and there are plans to set up more heavy industry, with more oil refineries, an iron and steel plant, and car assembly factories.

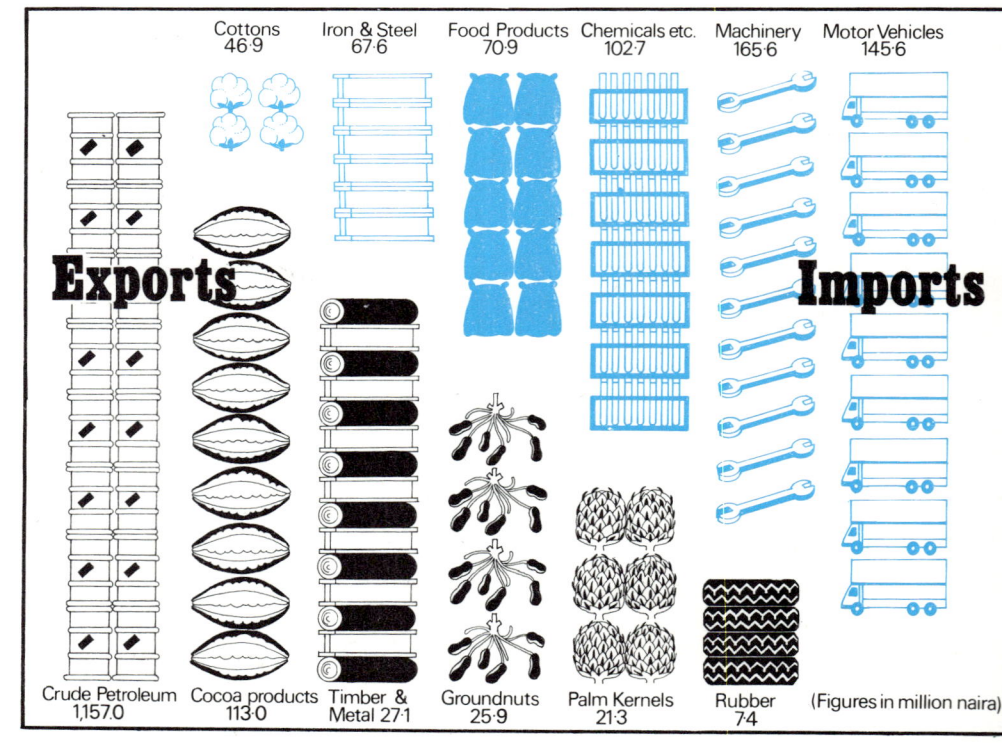

Exports: Crude Petroleum 1,157.0 · Cocoa products 113.0 · Timber & Metal 27.1 · Groundnuts 25.9 · Palm Kernels 21.3 · Rubber 7.4

Imports: Cottons 46.9 · Iron & Steel 67.6 · Food Products 70.9 · Chemicals etc. 102.7 · Machinery 165.6 · Motor Vehicles 145.6 · (Figures in million naira)

58

The growth of industry

Growth of Industry and Gross National Product 1967–1973 (figures in million naira)

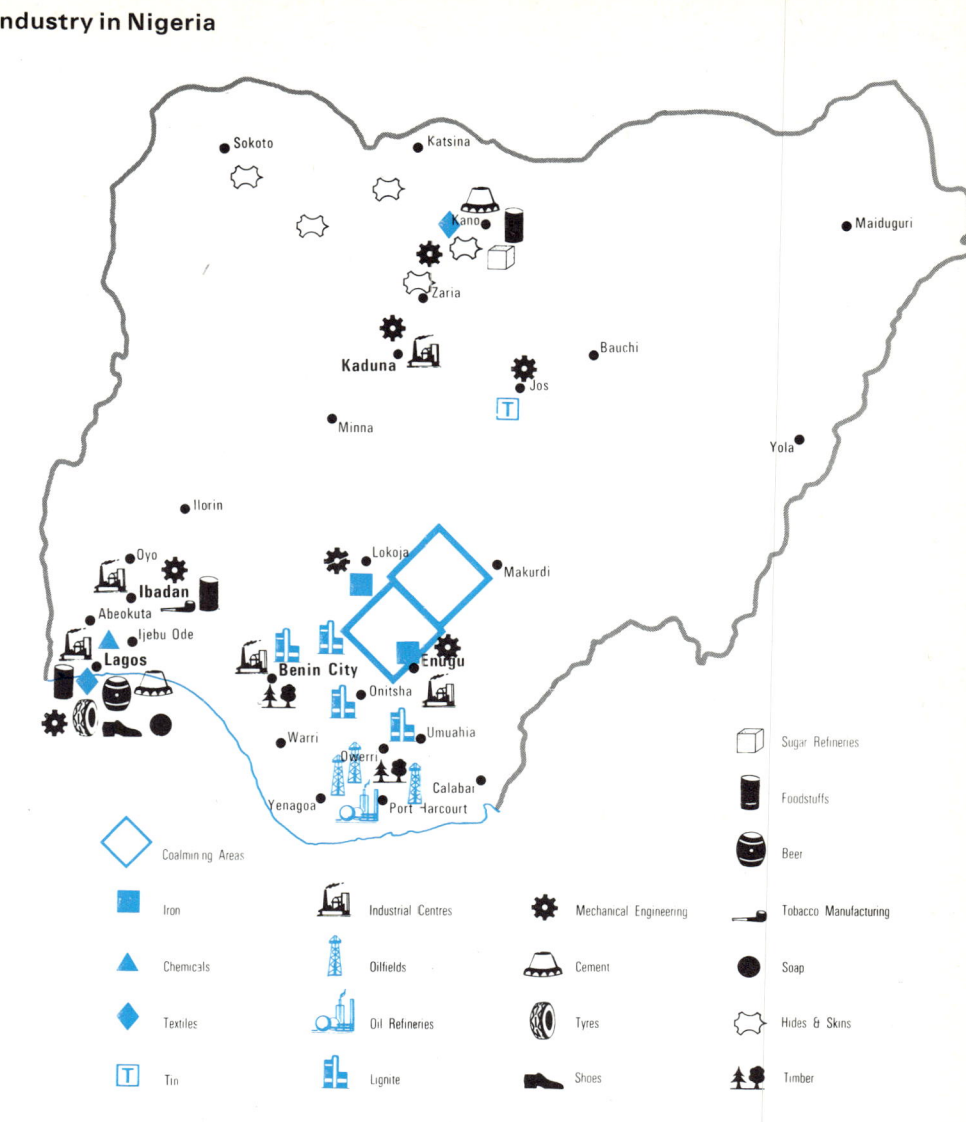

Industry in Nigeria

Map labels: Sokoto, Katsina, Kano, Maiduguri, Zaria, Bauchi, Kaduna, Jos, Minna, Yola, Ilorin, Oyo, Lokoja, Makurdi, Ibadan, Abeokuta, Ijebu Ode, Benin City, Enugu, Lagos, Onitsha, Warri, Umuahia, Owerri, Calabar, Yenagoa, Port Harcourt

Bar chart (each pair '67 and '73):
- Agriculture 1,582 / 1,735
- Mining 210 / 860
- Manufacturing 222 / 393
- Construction 160 / 340
- Communications 142 / 166
- Education 111 / 126

'67 '73 '67 '73 '67 '73 '67 '73 '67 '73 '67 '73

The spectacular growth rate in the economy is entirely due to the increase in petroleum production, which has stimulated development activity to a high level.

Map legend:
- Coalmining Areas
- Iron
- Chemicals
- Textiles
- Tin
- Industrial Centres
- Oilfields
- Oil Refineries
- Lignite
- Mechanical Engineering
- Cement
- Tyres
- Shoes
- Sugar Refineries
- Foodstuffs
- Beer
- Tobacco Manufacturing
- Soap
- Hides & Skins
- Timber

The labour force

- 56% Farmers, Fishermen, Hunters, etc
- 15% Sales Workers
- 12% Craftsmen and Production Workers
- 4% Service and Sport Workers
- 2% Professions
- 1.5% Transport Workers
- 1% Clerical Workers
- .07% Miners

+ 8.43% In Other Forms Of Work

Social factors of development

Since 1965 many of Nigeria's industries have at least doubled their output, and doubled their number of employees, while the numbers of clerical and office staff have increased several times over.

Despite this expansion there is growing unemployment and the beginnings of industrial unrest, with workers more organized in trade unions. With the high rate of inflation in 1974 the Government was forced to increase lower incomes by 100%, but this did not prevent widespread strikes in early 1975.

For the lower income groups the impact of inflation has been felt the hardest, with many items more than twice as expensive in 1973 as they were in 1960.

Cities have expanded at such a pace that the provision of modern facilities has fallen seriously behind. The lure of wealth in the towns has led to social problems. The educational system is one of Africa's best but is proving unsuited to Nigeria's real needs. School-leavers find themselves without work, but they are unwilling to go into agriculture, where they are most needed.

59

Gazetteer

Aba (5 10N 7 19E). Busy market and industrial town in East-Central State.

Abeokuta (7 0N 3 23E). Large market town in Western State, famous for its shrines and the Olumo Rock.

Adamawa (North-East State). A plateau area stretching into neighbouring Cameroon.

Argungu (12 55N 4 30E). Site of traditional fishing festival near Sokoto, North-Western State.

Badagry (6 25N 2 55E) Lagos State. A former slave-trade port founded in the 1700s. Accessible from the city of Lagos.

Bauchi (10 30N 9 45E). Busy and traditional Hausa town with old mosque.

Benin (6 20N 5 31E). Ancient capital of the powerful Benin empire. Ruins and palaces remain, but the city is developing as a modern administrative, industrial and university centre and capital of Mid-Western State.

Benue river. Nigeria's second river, navigable to the Cameroon border when in full flood.

Bida (9 2N 6 12E). Main town of the Nupe people and important craft centre, specialising in glass, brass and iron.

Birnin Kudu (12 32N 4 12E). Site of prehistoric rock paintings, Kano State.

Bonny (4 25N 7 13E). Old eighteenth century slave port, now an oil terminal.

Borgu Game Reserve (Kwara State). Well populated with wildlife but not yet developed as tourist centre.

Calabar (4 59N 8 23E). An important trading centre in the 18th and 19th centuries. Now developing as a modern centre.

Chad. The great lake on Nigeria's north-eastern edge. Fluctuating waters full of papyrus islands and wonderful wildlife. Hot climate. 800 ft above sea level.

Enugu (6 35N 7 30E). Founded as a commercial and industrial centre after the discovery of coal early this century. Abandoned during the Civil War but now an active State capital.

Esie (Kwara State). Site of hundreds of mysterious stone carvings about 200 years old.

Ibadan (7 40N 3 50E). Busy commercial and administrative centre referred to as the largest 'native city' in Africa. As capital of a powerful Yoruba state it was already a big city before colonisation. University town.

Ife (7 30N 4 31E). Founded in the 8th century AD and the spiritual home of all Yorubas. Now commercial centre and university town.

Ikom (6 0N 8 42E). Site of mysterious carved monoliths in forest groves.

Ikot Ekpene (5 12N 7 40E). Lively centre of arts and crafts in South-Eastern State.

Ilorin (8 30N 4 23E). Market town recently upgraded to State capital. A meeting place for north and south.

Jebba (9 9N 4 48E). An important crossing point on the Niger river with a fine bridge. Market town in Kwara State.

Jos (9 53N 8 51E). Expanding modern town and popular holiday centre with pleasant climate and rocky hill surroundings. Good museum. Tin mining and commercial centre.

Kaduna (10 5N 8 10E). Former capital of Northern Region established by the British. Textiles and other industries.

Kainji dam (Kwara State). Nigeria's main source of hydroelectric power, completed in 1969. Forms a large lake of 500 square miles on the Niger river.

Kano (11 58N 8 20E). Largest traditional Hausa city, with 11-mile wall, mud architecture, dye-pits, old market for trans-Saharan trade and huge mosque. Also a modern administrative, commercial and industrial centre. International airport.

Katsina (13 0N 7 35E). Ancient Hausa town with striking traditional architecture and impressive festivals.

Kontagora (10 23N 5 27E) North-Western State. A strategic town founded during the Fulani wars. The unpopulated savannah to the south has much wildlife.

Lagos (6 20N 3 20E). Main commercial, administrative and industrial centre of Nigeria, with the country's largest port at Apapa. It has grown rapidly from a population of a few thousand in 1900 to well over a million today. The city comprises the islands of Lagos, Victoria and Ikoyi, as well as the mainland districts of Ebute-Metta, Yaba, Surulere and Apapa.

Lokoja (7 48N 6 43E). Market town on the confluence of the Niger and Benue rivers. Port and potential iron-ore mining centre.

Maiduguri (12 0N 13 5E). Old traditional Kwara market town and seat of traditional Borno power. Becoming rapidly modernised.

Makurdi (7 43N 8 28E). Attractive town on the Benue river. Centre of the Tiv people.

Mambila plateau (North East State). Beautiful mountain scenery on the Cameroon border.

Niger river. For the final third of its 2,600 miles this river passes through Nigeria. The river delta is a massive complex of forested and swampy islands.

Nsukka (7 0N 7 50E). University town, West Central State.

Obudu (South East State). A pleasant and hilly holiday resort with refreshing climate.

Ogbomosho (8 5N 4 10E). Important Yoruba town with a large market. Cloth-weaving centre.

Onitsha (6 8N 6 55E). Important market town damaged during the Civil War but now revived. In East-Central State.

Oron (4 48N 8 14E). Interesting museum town with Ibibio and Efik cultural influence.

Oshogbo (7 55N 4 50E). Traditional Yoruba town famous as a cultural, artistic and religious centre, with shrines and a museum. Also a centre of the cocoa trade. Western State.

Oturkpo (7 10N 8 15E) Benue-Plateau State. Main town of the Idoma people.

Owerri (5 29N 7 0E). Large market town.

Oyo (7 58N 3 59E). An important traditional Yoruba town built in the 19th century to replace Old Oyo as the Yoruba capital.

Pankshin (9 25N 9 25E). A beautiful tourist centre in the rocky hills of the Jos plateau.

Pategi (8 50N 5 45E). Site of popular annual festival and regatta on the Niger River.

Port Harcourt (4 45N 7 20E). Large and modern city thriving as a result of the oil industry. Nigeria's second port.

Sapele (5 50N 5 40E). Important centre of the timber trade and port in Mid-Western State.

Sokoto (13 3N 5 15E). Influential centre of Islamic learning and authority for the Sahel region. Administrative capital. Hot dry climate.

Umuahia (5 33N 7 29E). Commercial town in East Central State. Ojukwu's temporary capital for rebel operations during the Civil War.

Warri (5 35N 5 57E). Booming oil town and port in Mid-West State.

Yankari Game Reserve (North East State). Nigeria's foremost centre of wildlife for the tourist industry, with pleasant warm springs for bathing. Lions, leopards, elephants and antelopes etc.

Yelwa (10 49N 8 41E). Pleasant small town and fishing centre on the Niger river, North-West State.

Yola (9 10N 12 37E). Important market town near the Cameroon border, North-East State.

Zaria (11 0N 7 25E). Ancient Hausa town in North-Central State, with traditional architecture. Commerce, industry and a university

The Twelve States of Nigeria

State	Capital	Area (sq. miles)
Lagos	Lagos	1,381
Western	Ibadan	29,100
Mid-Western	Benin City	14,922
Rivers	Port Harcourt	6,985
East-Central	Enugu	11,548
South-Eastern	Calabar	10,951
Benue-Plateau	Jos	39,204
Kwara	Ilorin	28,672
North-Western	Sokoto	65,143
North-Central	Kaduna	27,108
Kano	Kano	16,630
North-Eastern	Maiduguri	105,025

Index

Numbers in **heavy** type refer to illustrations.

Achebe, Chinua 20, **21**
Adekunle, Brigadier Benjamin (The Black Scorpion) **49**
African Unity, Organisation of 12, 47
Agbada (Yoruba gown) 16
Agriculture, decline of 52
Airports 13, 36
Akenzua II, Oba of Benin **40**
Akwete cloth 34
Alexandra, Princess **46**
All-Africa Games **19**
Ambrose, District Commissioner **44**
Ancestors, worship of 24
Apapa port **38**
Arabic language **21**
Arabic types 8
Arabs 12
Archery 18
Aro 42
Art treasures 12, **33**, 34
Asoi-oke (Yoruba turban) **17**
Athletics 19
Ayo **18**
Azikiwe, Nnamdi 44, **46**, 48

Balafon **32**, 32
Balewa, Sir Abubakar Tefewa **49**
Bananas **30**, 30
Bangles, glass 34
Barth **43**
Bantu 20, **41**
Basketball 19
Benin 8, 12, **15, 17,** 22, **25,** 33, 34, **35, 38,** 40, **40, 41,** 43, **43, 44, 45,** 48
Benin bronzes **12,** 33, **41**
Benin mask **24**
Benue river 8, **11**
Biafra 46, **47,** 52
Bida 34, **35**
Bini 40
Borno 40, 48
Bowharp **32**
Boxing 18
'Brazilian quarter', Lagos 38
Bread 29
Bride-price 14, **26**
Britain 8, 10, 12, 19, 22, 36, 42, **44**

Camels 36, **37,** 39
Camel market **29**
Canoes 36, **36**
Card games **51**
Carvings **8**
Cassava **30,** 30
Cattle 9, 10, **15**
Chad, lake 8
Children 14, 36, 47
'Chop bars' 30
Christianity 24, **25,** 26, 45
Chukwu, Ibo god 43
Civil war 8, 46, 49, 52
Clapperton, Hugh 43, **43**
Coastal area 10, **11**
Commerce 12

Corruption 46, 49
Costume, national **16,** 16
Crafts, practical **23**
Craftsmanship 34, **34,** 35
Cricket 19

Dancing **33, 51**
Dan Kano **48**
Dan Katsina **48**
Delta of the Niger 10, **10,** 44, 53
Denham **43**
Drumming **18,** 18, **20,** 32, **32,** 33
Dyeing **34, 34**

Edo **9**
Efik 40
Egypt, ancient 40
Eko Bridge **37**
Ekoi stone figure **24**
English language 20, **21,** 39
Equiano, Olaudah 42
Europeans 8, 10, 12, **16,** 18, 22, **23,** 24, 34, 40, **42,** 42, 44, 53
Ewuare, King of Benin 48
Explorers, European 43, **43,** 44
Eyo Festival 19

Facial markings **27**
Factories, new 52
Family, extended 14, 26, 51, **51**
Farming 10, **14**
Festivals 19, **19,** 26
Fish **30,** 30
Flute **32**
Football 18, **19**
Fulani **8, 9,** 10, **15, 17,** 24, 26, **41,** 43

Gelede mask **24**
Ghosts 26
Gods 24, **25**
Gold 42
Gowan, General Yakubu **12,** 46, **47, 52**
Groundnuts (peanuts) **12, 30,** 30, 31
Groundnut stew **30,** 30

Habe Tower **35**
Haile Selassie **52**
Hairstyles **16, 17, 34**
Hamitic types 8
Handshake **26**
Hare, stories of 48
Hausa **8, 9,** 12, **16,** 16, **17,** 20, 21, **26,** 39, 40, **41,** 46, 48
Head, loads carried on **36**
'High Life' 32

Ibadan **9,** 22, **23, 28,** 39, **41,** 43, **44**
Ibo **8,** 8, **9, 16,** 20, **21, 27,** 34, 40, 42, 44, 46, 77
Ibibio **9,** 40, **45**
Ife 8, 33, 40
Ikere Ekiti, Yorubaland 44
Ilorin **16, 44**
Income groups, gaps between 52
Independence, October 1960 46, **46**
Islam 8, 22, 24, **25,** 33, 40, **41,** 43
Ivory 10, 12, 34, 42

Jester **24**
Jos Museum 35
Jos Plateau **10,** 10, **11, 44**

Kaduna **35**
Kainji Dam 43
Kanem-Borno empire 8, 12, **41**
Kano **2-3,** 12, **13,** 22, **25, 27, 29, 33, 34, 35, 36, 38,** 38, **41,** 44
Kanuri **8, 9, 16,** 20
Kofar Motta Gate, Kano **39**
Kurmi Market, Kano 39

Lagos **9, 11, 15,** 19, **19,** 22, **29, 37, 38,** 39, 41, 44, **45,** 52
Land, reclaimed 38
Lander brothers 10, 43, **43**
Leatherwork 35
Left hand **26**
Lorries 29
Lugard, Frederick 44, **45**

Malnutrition 47
'Mammy wagons' 36, **37**
Mangrove swamps 10, **11**
Markets **6, 29**
'Market mammies' 28
Marriage 14, 26
Massacres of Ibos 46
Meat 30, 31
Medical students **23**
'Medusa' hairstyle **17**
Men, domestic idleness of 53
Migrations into Nigeria 8, 41, **41**
Missionaries 43, **43,** 44
Mosques **25**
Mosaic 35
Mud buildings 39
Mungo Park **43**
Music **32,** 32
Musicians **29, 33**
Muslims 13, **17,** 25

Naira **28**
National Youth Service Corps 22
Neolithic axes 8
New Nigerian newspaper **35**
Newspapers 20, 37
Niger River **10,** 10, **11, 36,** 43, 44
Nigerian Airways 36, **36**
Nkrumah, Kwame **49**
Nok culture 8, 33, **40, 41**
Nupe **9,** 34
Nyerere, Julius **52**

Obas of Benin 40
Oil 12, **13,** 38, 52, 53
Ojukwu, Lt. Col. 46, **47**
Oron Museum 35
Ostentation 51
Oudney **43**
Overcrowding in cities 52
Oyo 43

Palm wine 30
Palm Wine Drunkard, The 26
Pidgin 21, 32
Polo 19
Portuguese 38, 42
Pottery **35**
Protectorates 44

Railways 36
Rain forest 10, **11**
Ransome-Kuti, Fela **32**
Regional power groups 46
Restaurants 30
Rice **30,** 30
Roads 36, 38
Rock paintings 8
Royal Niger Company 44

Sabon Gari, Kano 39
Sahara 10, **12,** 12, 38, **42,** 42, 43, 44
Sahel semi-desert 10, 40
Sallah Festival **17**
Savannah 10, **11,** 32, 40
Saxophone 32
Schools system 22, **22,** 43
Sewing **23**
Shanty towns 38, **38**
Slaves 10, **12,** 12, 38, **42,** 42, 43, 44
Slave routes **42**
Snacks, sold in street **31**
Soil erosion, danger of 53
Sokoto, Sultan of 26
Soyinka, Wole 20, **49**
Spices 30, 42
Spider, stories of 48
Spirits, worship of 24
Stability, search for 52
States, 12 new 46, **47,** 51
Story-telling 18, **48**
Suburban home **15**
Swimming 18

Tailoring 16
Teachers 22, 23
Television **20**
Tennis 19
Tetse fly 10
Textiles **29, 35**
Tiv **9, 20,** 48
Tortoise, stories of 48
Tourists **52**
Town families **15**
Traffic jams **37,** 38
Trance **33**
Trains 36
Tribes 8, 24, 27
Tribalism, and the family 50
Tutuola, Amos 26
Twins 26, **27**

Water supply **15**
Weaving 34, **35**
Wedding **17, 45**
West Indies 42
Witchcraft **27**
Wives, plurality of (polygymy) 14
Wrestling 18
Writers 20
Wood carving 34, **34**
Wood shortage, danger of 53
World War II 44

Ughelli, oil rig at **53**
Universities 22, **22**

Yams **30,** 30
Yoruba **8,** 8, **9,** 16, **16, 17,** 20, **21,** 26, **27,** 32, 34, 38, 40, **41,** 43, 44, 46, 48

Zaria **11,** 22, **51**

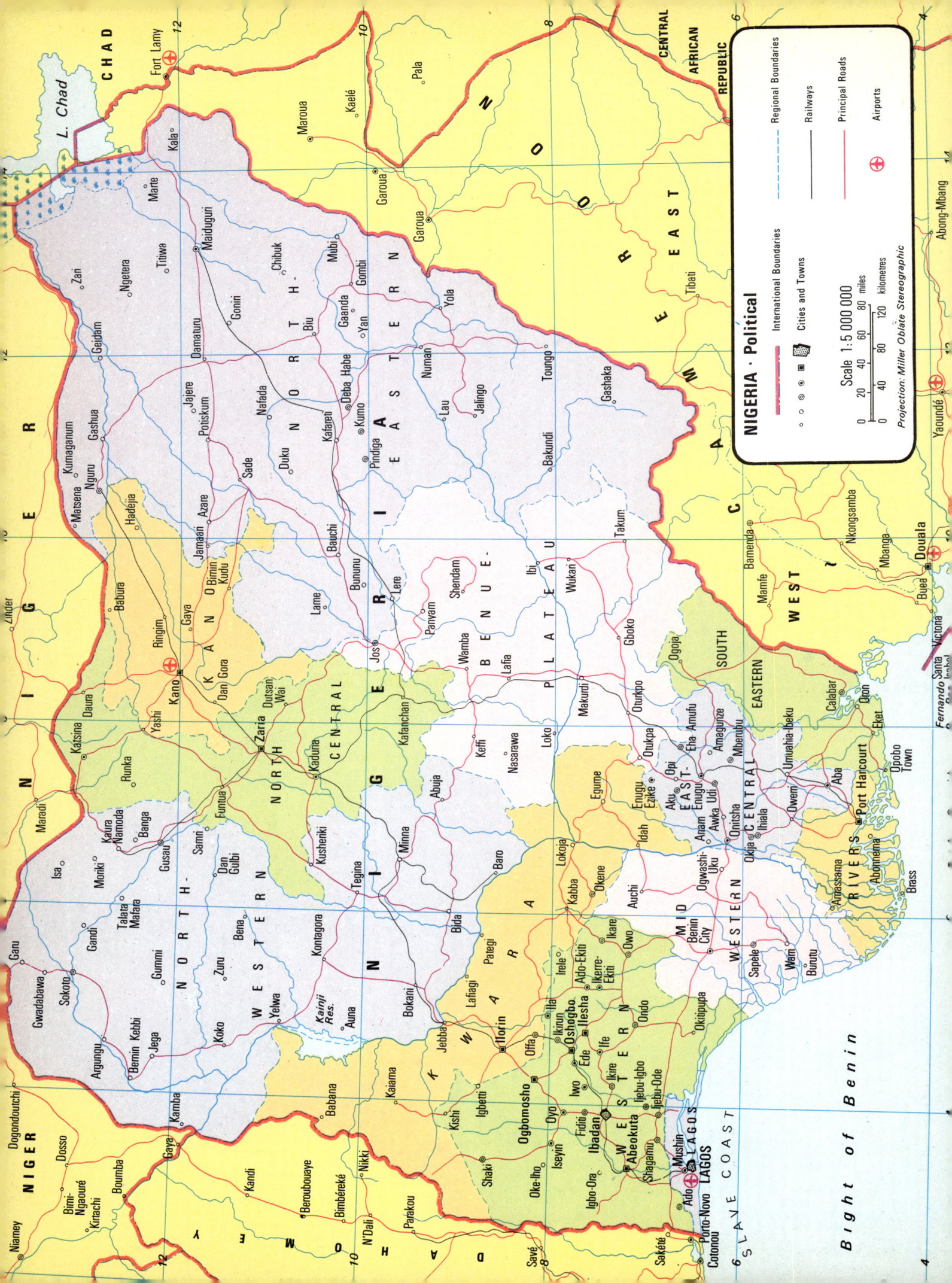

NIGERIA · Political

		Regional Boundaries
		Railways
		Principal Roads
		Airports

International Boundaries
Cities and Towns

Scale 1:5 000 000

miles
0 20 40 60 80
0 40 80 120
kilometres

Projection: Miller Oblate Stereographic

Labels and place names visible on the map

NIGER · **CHAD** · L. Chad · L. Chad · Fort Lamy

CAMEROUN · WEST · EAST · SOUTH · CENTRAL AFRICAN REPUBLIC

NIGERIA (regions): NORTH-EASTERN · KANO · NORTH-CENTRAL · NORTH-WESTERN · BENUE-PLATEAU · KWARA · WESTERN · MID-WESTERN · EAST-CENTRAL · RIVERS · SOUTH-EASTERN · LAGOS

Maroua · Kaélé · Pala · Garoua · Garoua · Tibati · Abong-Mbang · Yaoundé · Mbanga · Douala · Buea · Victoria · Fernando Santa Isabel

Zan · Kala · Marte · Ngetera · Titiwa · Maiduguri · Chibuk · Mubi · Gombi · Gonini · Biu · Gaanda · Y'an · Yola · Numan · Toungo · Gashaka · Bakundi · Lau · Jalingo · Takum · Mamfe · Bamenda · Nkongsamba · Mbanga

Geidam · Damaturu · Jajere · Potiskum · Nafada · Sade · Duku · Deba Habe · Kumo · Kafareti · Pindiga · Bauchi · Bununu · Lame · Lere · Shendam · Panyam · Wamba · Ibi · Wukari · Gboko · Ogoja · Takum

Gashua · Nguru · Kumaganum · Matsena · Hadejia · Azare · Janaari · Bimin Kudu · Gaya · Ringim · Kano · Dan Gora · Dutsan Wai · Kaduna · Kafanchan · Keffi · Abuja · Nasarawa · Loko · Makurdi · Otukpo · Oturkpo · Idah · Egume · Opi · Eha Amufu · Amagunze · Mbenubu · Umuahia-Ibeku

Daura · Katsina · Runka · Yashi · Zaria · Funtua · Minna · Kushenki · Tegina · Baro · Lokoja · Kabba · Okene · Auchi · Enugu Ezike · Aku · Udi · Enugu · Awka · Onitsha · Anam · Ihiala · Owem · Aba · Oron · Calabar · Eket

Maradi · Kaura Namoda · Banga · Sarni · Dan Gulbi · Gusau · Kontagora · Bida · Pategi · Ogwashi-Uku · Benin City · Ikare · Owo · Ondo · Sapele · Warri · Burutu · Abonema · Brass · Arrassama · Opobo Town · Port Harcourt

Isa · Moriki · Talata Mafara · Gandi · Gummi · Bena · Zuru · Kainji Res. · Auna · Bokani · Lafiagi · Ilorin · Offa · Ila · Ilkirun · Oshogbo · Ilesha · Ife · Ado-Ekiti · Ikerre-Ekiti · Irele · Iwo · Ede · Ikire · Jebu-Igbo · Jebu-Ode · Okitipupa

Ganu · Gwadabawa · Sokoto · Jega · Argungu · Birnin Kebbi · Koko · Yelwa · Kamba · Gaya · Babana · Kaiama · Kishi · Igbetti · Ogbomosho · Oyo · Fidiri · Ibadan · Iseyin · Oke-Iho · Shaki · Igbo-Ora · Abeokuta · Shagamu · Mushin · LAGOS · Ado

Niamey · Bimi-Ngaouré · Kirachi · Dosso · Boumba · Dogondoutchi · N'Dali · Parakou · Bimbéréké · Beroubouaye · Nikki · Kandi · Save · Cotonou · Porto-Novo · Sakété · Zinder

DAHOMEY · Slave Coast · **Bight of Benin**